'I could not put this book down ...  had me laughing out loud in places, and reduced me to wrenching sobs in others ... [A] refreshingly honest book'
— *City Press*

'Ultimately you should read this book not only because it is an important one, but also because it is a bloody good read. Adam Levin invites the reader into his life in this book, paying tribute to the immense human suffering that illness causes, but also reminding the reader that it is possible to survive with your personality intact' — *Cape Times*

'[A] story of courage, of illumination'   — *Pretoria News*

'[A]n insightful survivor's message'   — *Drum*

'Although I initially expected a depressingly gloomy book, I was pleasantly surprised by it — *Aidsafari* is a brave book detailing one person's fight for survival, and how he faces the harshness and beauty of this roller-coaster called life ... Refreshing and highly inspirational, Adam Levin's memoir is filled with hope'
— *Big Issue*

'Adam Levin ... brings his fierce spirit to the account but also mixes it with a moving, but never maudlin, honesty and vulnerability. An extraordinary achievement, not least because it inspires rather than depresses'   — *Farmers Weekly*

'Like its author, *Aidsafari* is ... the most engaging sermon and redemption song in secular literature right now'
— *Sunday Times*

'It is outrageous, it is open, it is honest, it is intelligent, it makes you cry, it makes you laugh, it won't let you go, it reaches the heart and it reaches the brain'   — *The Teacher*

ADAM LEVIN IS A gay South African author, journalist, fashionista and occasional cultural terrorist. A winner of two Mondi Gold Awards for Journalism, he trained as a staffer for *Style* magazine, before travelling through some twenty African countries. These journeys resulted in a hugely popular collection, *The Wonder Safaris*, published by Struik in 2003. His next book, *The Art of African Shopping*, published in 2005, details his adventures as a trader and explores the magic of African crafts, fashion, food and music. This is his third, and most personal book.

AIDSAFARI

A Memoir of My Journey with Aids

Adam Levin

My sincere thanks to my editor, Robert Plummer, for his skill and sensitivity in editing this text, and to my publisher, Marlene Fryer at Zebra Press, for her commitment to this contaminated memoir. Another big thank you to Merwelene van der Merwe and Carl Collison for their powerful photographic images. Adam Levin

Published by Zebra Press
an imprint of Struik Publishers
(a division of New Holland Publishing (South Africa) (Pty) Ltd)
PO Box 1144, Cape Town, 8000
New Holland Publishing is a member of Johnnic Communications Ltd

www.zebrapress.co.za

First published 2005

3 5 7 9 10 8 6 4 2

Publication © Zebra Press 2005
Text © Adam Levin 2005

Back cover photograph: Merwelene van der Merwe
Photograph on pages 104–105: Carl Collison

All rights reserved. No part of this publication may be reproduced, stored in a retrieval system or transmitted, in any form or by any means, electronic, mechanical, photocopying, recording or otherwise, without the prior written permission of the copyright owners.

PUBLISHING MANAGER: Marlene Fryer
EDITOR: Robert Plummer
PROOFREADER: Ronel Richter-Herbert
COVER AND TEXT DESIGNER: Natascha Adendorff-Olivier
TYPESETTER: Monique van den Berg
PRODUCTION MANAGER: Valerie Kömmer

Set in 11 pt on 14 pt Bembo

Reproduction by Hirt & Carter (Cape) (Pty) Ltd
Printed and bound by Paarl Print, Oosterland Street, Paarl, South Africa

ISBN 1 86872 928 1

For Mom and Dad.

How on earth did I find you?

PREFACE

I HAVE NO IDEA HOW long I have been HIV-positive, maybe five years, maybe less, maybe more, but I have had Aids for the past two years. When I disclosed my status to my parents they assured me that I wouldn't have to worry about the cost of treatment and that they would remain at my side on the journey that lay ahead. Few people are so blessed. The majority of people with Aids struggle not only with the disease, but with its exorbitant financial pressures and cruel social stigmas. I have suffered none of that. I have not been shunned by the people around me (okay, maybe a couple, and you know who you are); I have not had to worry about access to anti-retrovirals; and I have been surrounded with love and care. And yet, this has undoubtedly been the most difficult journey of my life. If you'd asked me, in the beginning, if I'd be able to handle the degree of suffering and uncertainty that lay ahead of me, I wouldn't have hesitated in my response. 'No, it's far too much,' I'd have said. 'Hand me the revolver.'

But I didn't know. With the generation before me already tragically lost, my own generation had buried its head in the sand. I read daily about Aids in the newspaper. I knew the extent of its spread and had some grasp on the politics of the crusade to manage it. And yet, despite being gay, thirty years old, and a resident of the country with the highest infection rate in the world, I was completely ignorant about the realities of this disease. I was bang in the epicentre of the Aids pandemic, and yet, if you'd asked me what Aids was really about on a daily basis, I wouldn't have known what to say. I had no sense of the experience of the progression of this disease. I was clueless as to the degree of pain and anxiety involved. Like so many of us, I was a victim of the secrecy and ignorance surrounding what has become the world's most pressing concern.

Often while writing this memoir, I lost faith in its process. I wrestled with the egotism of writing sixty thousand words about myself, and I doubted its value. Many times, I abandoned the whole idea. But as unfortunate as the story of my suffering might be, the circumstances surrounding it have been extremely fortunate. The angels of care and affirmation have always been close at hand, and whatever doubts I still might have as to the significance of this manuscript, if there is any way I can express the depth of my gratitude for that support, it is by telling a story. And this is it.

When I first got sick, I looked for books that might prepare me for the journey ahead of me. I looked in the bookstores, I surfed Amazon, and yet I found nothing. This was no accident. In its own insidious way, the conspiracy to keep this disease walled in silence had triumphed. If this memoir helps to chip away at a single brick of that immense wall of silence, I will be greatly honoured. If my story can be of any solace or assistance to anyone battling the rigours of this disease, or to any of the people close to him or her, it will be my privilege to offer that. But this is not intended as a handbook for people with Aids: on a deeper, more intimate level, it is simply a story about lostness and love and life and how rarely it fails to surprise you.

At times, I also struggled with the fears of personal exposure and worthlessness surrounding the publication of this book. But when I finally accepted that this unextraordinary story was possibly one worth sharing, finishing this book proved one of the easiest things I'd ever done. It proved a far less complicated endeavour than either of the collections of journalism I had published or the novel I was working on – the characters of which would yank me out of bed at 4:30 in the morning, demanding that I hobble over to my laptop and inform them where on earth I was leading them.

In the end, there is nothing simpler than telling a story when it is yours alone.

Probably the trickiest part in the whole written journey was choosing a title. I knew that I wanted to make this memoir as accessible as possible, because, ultimately, if it didn't reach people there would have been little point in writing it. And yet everything I came up with seemed either so dumb-assed obvious or nauseatingly soppy, I couldn't imagine putting my name beneath it. And so I began bothering everyone around me for their responses to any vaguely possible option.

I'd been stuck on '2' for a while – my miserable, rock-bottom cell count when I first tested positive. It captured the tragedy of my own denial and the almost fatal progression of the HI virus within my body as a result of that process – at one point, 429 000 copies of itself within each tiny cell. '2' also evoked the idea of a second chance and a new beginning, but, as my darling friend Alex so astutely observed, '2' seemed glaringly inappropriate for a journey that had been so distinctly solo.

My editor had come up with the phrase 'Still Life with Aids'. I played with the words. 'Still! Life with Aids.' It captured the amazing resilience of my journey, the merciful possibility that one could have Aids and *still* be here. And yet there was something eerily frozen about the phrase. For this had been a journey from paralysis to gradual agility. A story about learning to walk again, to move, to do things for myself. A terrified crawl from the door of death back into the great wide world of life.

'Aids shmaids!' my friend Roy suggested. 'Yeah,' I figured. 'But that makes it sound like it's all been a big joke, but it hasn't; it's been fuckin' hectic!'

'There's your title,' Roy said. '*Fuckin' Hectic*.' It was pretty damned good, but still didn't quite capture a journey that had been so profoundly personal.

So I lay back and I thought. I reflected on all the miraculous but exhausting African journeys of wonder I had chronicled in my first book *The Wonder Safaris*. I thought of that beautifully lyrical Swahili word for journey: 'safari'. And I realised that the hardest, most frightening safari of all had been the one that had not required a single step. It had been the journey in my head and through every aching nerve in my body.

The journey inside.

I searched for a word that might capture that whole ghastly, life-changing experience for myself. But I found nothing, and finally I surrendered to the fact that there wasn't a single word in the dictionary that resonated something so uniquely personal for me. And then my mischievous little brain finally figured out that if no word existed, I would simply have to make one up. And then, from somewhere deep in my subconscious, it came to me.

Somehow the curious ring of such a strange, invented word seemed perfectly appropriate for the scary unfamiliarity of the journey I had scribbled down. Over and over I sung the word to myself, until I learnt to pronounce it not as two words, 'Aids Safari', but rather with all the faith-drenched, rhythmic resonance of the phrase that rung out from the thick, marijuana-puffin' haze of my adolescence: 'Jah Rastafari!' I loved the way the sound concluded itself so triumphantly on the letter 'I', which was, after all, where it had all begun, and where it all ultimately ended up. At I.

And so there you have it. As simply as a complicated lad like m'self could possibility put it: AIDSAFARI! A Memoir of My Journey with Aids.

This book is for all of you who were there; without you, it would not have had an author.

With big love,
Adamo.

PART ONE

GOOD MORNING
3 March 2004

I OPEN MY EYES AT 5 a.m. as usual, swig on my liquid morphine and tug at a cigarette. The liquid's supposed to work quickly, but it doesn't, and last night's dose is wearing off. Anyway, my feet aren't all that hideous this morning. I'm getting used to it now. If I keep the blankets off them and lie on my back, I'll be okay.

Six o'clock. Gotta move. My coccyx is aching. There's a dry, raw patch there from lying on my back all these months and there isn't much flesh between the skin and bone. I must lie on my side for a while – even with the sores there. It's my TV side. Months of gazing at that stupid box have worn the skin down and some little bumps have formed. They aren't bedsores yet, but I must keep an eye on them.

The TV's on as usual – my faithful, blaring companion. Sometimes I dream that none of this ever happened, but then I wake up and it's a few seconds before the pain reminds me. I hate that moment. But the glimmer of the TV eases its darkness. I wish I could sleep straight through, but I can't. I wake briefly every hour. It may be the medication. It may just be me. I blink my way through BBC News and pass out again.

Seven fifteen. Time for my morphine pills. The liquid doesn't work for long. If I take three pills now, I'm usually all right until 4 p.m. It's a slow release – every couple of hours I get a few milligrams of the blessed analgesia. The government says you can't take more than two of these per day, but the government ain't got nerve damage, I guess. I take eleven of the tiny purple ones daily and I still suffer a lot. These will take two hours to kick in. Half a cigarette. Asleep again by seven thirty. Awake by nine.

'No, I don't know what I want for breakfast, Mom. I don't think I can eat anything ... An egg? God no. I'll retch ... Fruit? All right, I'll try some. A bit later.'

Ten o'clock. I can sit upright now. Time for my morning's anti-retrovirals. I'm very good with these. In the past eight months, I've never missed a dose. The trick is, you gotta take them at the same time every day. Otherwise you die. Once I threw up and I had to swallow the whole bunch again. I really should eat before I take them, so I force down some fruit. Three big orange pills first – the plastic rugby ball ones. Then the white oval one – hate the oval, it always sticks. Now the other lot – the yellow one with its weird vanilla flavour. Uggh, the blues. The green oval one. Then the five little blue and yellows – they're the easiest, so I leave them till last. Done. I deserve another cigarette. Better lie down again. Feet aren't ready yet.

Ten thirty. I switch on my computer. I have been writing for half an hour now, spewing out these thoughts as fast as I can type, sipping on ginger beer to hold back the nausea. But it isn't working. Better lie down again. My red blood cells are being chomped up by the chemotherapy, so some days my strength is zero. Hopefully, I'll feel better later. I've got to get more than half an hour's work in today. As long as I can churn out something, I won't feel so useless.

But some days I can't.

EIGHT AND A HALF
6 April 2003

RIO DE JANEIRO. FOUR in the morning. Central bus terminus. I've just arrived by bus from Paraty down the coast. I knew we'd arrive at a ludicrous hour. They said we wouldn't but they lied. The sky is black ink and there are dodgy faces lurking around in the yellow light of the bus terminus. Gaudy bottle-blonde women sitting in their booths. 'Taxi!?' they shriek. I sit on my suitcase, unsure what to do. Shall I just hover here until morning or should I brave the streets and look for a hotel?

'No, lady! No taxi! I'm taking the bus, thank you. How do I get to Copacabana?'

The bus rattles through the dark night. The street lights catch the contours of mouldy, monumental concrete and the palm boulevard of Flamengo Bay. I have no idea where I'm going. A faint blue haze is creeping over the lush hills, scattered like mossy stalagmites through this bewildering city. They poke up into the skyline, menacing and beautiful. I have been here before – years ago – but I don't recognise much. The remainder of last night's drunks are stumbling along the Avenida de Nossa Senhora de Copacabana. 'Okay. Drop me here. There must be a hotel around. Obrigado.'

I struggle with the turnstile and attempt to drag my suitcase along the cracked pavement. Bump. Thump. Clunk. Narrow, yellow eyes in plank-thin alleyways. Of course, there's no hotel! I lug my goods up the stairs of a few garish, overpriced whorehouses. 'Yes, 100 rials, but you must be out by midday.'

'Midday? That's ludicrous. Oh Rio! I'm not looking for a place to fuck. I'm exhausted. I need to sleep. Is there nowhere cheaper?'

'Down the block. Third street on your left.'

'Okay. 'brigado.'

And so I trudge. Again and again, I land up at the same shitty little excuses for hotels. My vision is blurring from exhaustion. Eventually, I find something I can just afford. It looks clean enough, but it's full, so I'll have to wait until checkout time at eleven. I sit on the balcony and chew on a cigarette to keep me awake. The morning air is crisp and beautiful. People are blossoming from their apartments like frangipani flowers, walking their dogs, buying their newspapers. I watch them come and go and inhale the sweetness of their daily rituals.

Six thirty. 'Could I get something to eat in the meanwhile? ... Seven? Okay. I'll wait.' Fresh rolls, jam, some fruit and coffee. Feel better. I drape myself on the tattered, red leather sofa in the lobby and page through some predictable Portuguese tabloids. A few Brits and Germans trot down for breakfast. But no one's checking out. It's beautiful outside. I check in my luggage and head out for a stroll on the beachfront. I'm in Rio de Janeiro for God's sake. The most magical city on the planet.

It is already scorching as I make my way down to the promenade. Rio is waking up in all its splendour. The world stretches out along the undulating black and white mosaic of the sidewalk. Leathery old men in white Speedos. Hot Latino hunks jogging, with golden crucifixes thumping on their chests. Middle-aged women and teenage dogs.

Hardly anyone has much clothing on. I sit and watch. Yawning but exhilarated.

Eleven o'clock. Finally, I transfer my luggage to a grim little room with a too-low, too-short bed and no space to manoeuvre. The window opens onto a brick wall, and it's three times over my budget. I'm too excited to sleep. I strip down to my Speedo and some trainers and head back to the beach. There's a gay beach here somewhere, I'm told, but where? I stroll down the elegant curve of Copacabana and on to the radiant Ipanema – stations 10, 9, 8½. There it is – a giant rainbow flag fluttering weakly in the limp breeze. Around half the people here are gay, I guess. Dark, brooding boys with chiselled abs in bright, tight, box-cut swimsuits. Raven-haired carioca girls in Gucci sunglasses. I spread myself out on the sand and order a Coke. I'm home. I never want to leave.

And I don't – until five o'clock at least. I lie here, basted in coconut oil, baking in the magnificent Brazilian sunlight. I make eye contact with a few boys, but nothing serious. I don't mind. I feel sexy. Just lying here in paradise, perving. Pure delight.

There's a bunch of British tourists sitting nearby. Their conversation is upsetting me. One particular queen with a ponytail, Jackie O shades and a paunch is speaking far too loudly. 'What a gaw-juss boy that was last night. He really likes you, I think. Oooh yes. Has he called you? … Never mind, luv, we'll see him at the club tonight.'

Oh Margaret, I groan under my breath. Why do *you* have to be here? Why the leathery, middle-aged fags on a package tour, hunting for young brown boys who'll fuck 'em for a couple of hundred rials? Am I envious? Or — shudder — am I as pathetic as they are? Uggh. I don't want anyone. I'll just watch. Don't touch me. Don't come over and speak to me. And please shut up, Margaret.

Grrr. I don't think Margaret *can* shut up. She's found a new victim. 'Just been to Caraguatatuba, dahling. Pretty beach. And so easy to get there. You just hop down to the Rodovario and take the first bus, and there you are, sipping a coconut with some lovely brown boy. It's perfect. I mean, what more d'you want form a summer hol? … Oh, just take a look at that one, luv. Isn't that just delicious?'

Oh Mah-gah-ret! I hope I'm not like you. You give me stomach cramps. You know you'd never score meat like this back home, so you come here, with your traveller's cheques, and the boys gobble them up. You're just the queen of Ipa-fucking-nema, aren't you?

I tune in to the sound of the waves crashing, hoping it'll drown out the tedious banter, but it doesn't. I nibble on some grilled cheese on a stick. That's what they eat here. Grilled cheese.

This is my third time in Brazil. I visited briefly in the early nineties on a whistle-stop media tour, en route to Mexico, and saw and heard just enough to fall in love with the place and its music. I next spent two wonderful months here in 2002, scribbling notes on São Paulo Fashion Week, crashing glamorous parties and interviewing architects. I had come to spend time with my lover Marcos. It had been very special and I had hoped the affair would hold, but it hadn't. A year later there was a cool distance between us. We'd spent hours together, but since I'd got off the plane, we hadn't so much as touched each other. We'd lost something. Our *bossa nova*, I guess.

We spent countless nights in that insane tropical megalopolis, trying to recapture our magic. Listening to our favourite old songs, snorting cocaine in the bathrooms of greasy bodegas and dancing separately at nightclubs. We argued like miserable bitches in Paraty, and so I'd finally come to Rio, alone, determined to have myself a fine Brazilian time in spite of my disappointment. And, had it not been for Margaret's incessant bleating, sprawled out on a deck chair on 8½, I couldn't have been more content.

I make my way back to my horrible hotel room, smoke a joint and curl up on the too-short bed for a couple of hours, gazing at the lazy ceiling fan. Around nine, I step out to buy a slice of pizza and a pastry. The streets are a jungle of people, hurrying home from work and gulping down guarana smoothies from the streetside stalls. The traffic roars. My skin tingles with sunburn. Tight and clean amid the urban grime. I head home, dip into a shower and ready myself for my first night out.

I arrive much too early at Le Boy. There are a few beauties hanging around the thumping, cavernous dance floor. I cradle a beer and sit in a corner and perve. Some trash plonks himself down next to me. Looking for business, I figure. Cute enough, but he's drunk. He takes my hand, grins stupidly and rubs it on his hard cock. I pull away. He's slurring. His English is bad and the conversation is embarrassingly thin. 'You like me? I like you. You like this?

Is big, yes? Very big.' Yeah, great, it's big. I don't care. I can do better. I'm off to dance, I announce. He looks wounded, but I hurry off. When I spot him later, he just glares at me. He's glugging whiskies with an elderly tourist. Oh how quickly they've found love! I'm happy for them.

Le Boy fills up fast. The fashion is kicking, and the bronzed boys shaking it on the dance floor are kicking it even harder. I strike up a rapport with a short young queen in alternative garb. He's cute. I bend down and we kiss. We fondle a little on the dance floor, but something holds me back. Around 2 a.m., I announce I'm leaving and arrange to meet him at the beach the following day. Oh fuck, am I turning into Margaret?

The following morning he arrives, looking more feminine and awkward in the daylight. The conversation fizzles after a few minutes. I can't think of anything to say. Somehow, I don't think this is a healthy relationship. Perhaps I am turning into Margaret.

Over the following week, I see no reason to alter my routine. I make the odd expeditions to buildings I want to see. One morning I take the cranky bus over the bridge to Niteroi and clamber up the coast road to where Oscar Niemeyer's modernist spaceship of an art gallery hovers on the edge of the cliff, ready to take off into the azure sky. I can count on one hand the times I've been so moved by a building. The Grand Mosque at Djenne in Mali; the moss-stained coral Omani mansions in Zanzibar; the Chrysler in New York ... But by midday I find myself scurrying helplessly back to Ipanema, placing myself in the same spot and perving. It's glorious. And my tan is coming along nicely.

I have lost some serious blubber, as people keep telling me, but I'm delighted. I check out my lean, brown frame in the hotel mirror and feel sexy. I buy a cheery green and yellow Brazil T-shirt which glows against my skin. Off to Le Boy again. Look, but don't touch.

And so it continues, for seven days. I could keep at it, but I'm anxious to get back to São Paulo for Skol Beats – a two-day techno music festival. I smoke a joint with Marcos when I arrive. We laugh and philosophise a little, but no flame rekindles. Besides, he has just taken on a new full-time job, and I am to spend my days cooped up in the apartment, gazing at the parking lot across the street. He can't afford the ticket for Skol Beats, he claims. Another disappointment. How nice.

I spend a week in São Paulo, simmering. I trudge up and down among the office blocks of Avenida Paulista, dipping into CD stores to expand my Brazilian music collection, but this is a business city, and everyone's at the office except me. After a few days hanging aimlessly around the shopping malls, I'm done. Fuck it, I figure. Who am I kidding? The relationship is ova! O.V.A! The least I can do is get home before my tan fades.

HOME

25 April 2003

ARRIVING IN JOHANNESBURG IS a relief. I see my people – Roy, Alex, Katy – and go to dinner at Mom and Dad's. Everyone comments on my tan and I'm chuffed. I begin a new job, working for a daily newspaper that is set to launch in a few months. Because the product is still in its planning stages, the job is not particularly demanding. Some days I'm not sure what I'm supposed to be doing. I play CDs on my computer and watch my tan fade. I feel some pain in my feet at times, but winter is coming. It's circulation or something, I guess.

Over the past few months, my parents' domestic worker, Elsie, has been losing weight. Now she's started coughing. They have beseeched her to see a doctor, but she says it's not necessary. Eventually the coughing gets so bad, Mom bundles her in the car and takes her to our GP, who tests her for tuberculosis. The tests are positive. Elsie must start a course of medication, but she doesn't want to. There's nothing wrong with her, she says. Privately, the doctor tells Mom he's sure Elsie has Aids and should be tested immediately. But Elsie refuses. She also refuses to take the TB medicine.

I offer Elsie a lift to the bus stop one afternoon and we chat a little in the car. She seems thin, though not desperately so. She is bright, attractive and in her late thirties. I don't broach the subject of her illness. We talk of her family and her recent trip to her home in Limpopo Province. But, as the weeks pass, Elsie gets sicker. She cannot work, but lies coughing in her bed. Eventually she moves to her sister's house in the township so she can be taken care of. She still says there's nothing wrong with her. Mom calls the township. Elsie is doing okay, they report. Slim and sexy, like me.

A few days later, I get a call from Dad. 'Hi Boy. How are you doing …?'

I like it when he calls me Boy.

'Listen, we thought you were looking particularly skeletal. Won't you please indulge us and go and see a doctor for a check-up. A full medical. Don't worry about the money, I'll pay for it. Won't you go?'

I'm angry. There's nothing wrong with me. I'm looking great, for God's sake. How dare they impose this? How dare they infer there's something the matter. Invasion of the Parents!

'I'm not sure, Dad,' I grumble weakly. 'I'll think about it.'

Over the following week, I do think about it. In fact, I think of little else. I have thought and thought about this for the past five years and I've never done anything about it. To tell you the truth, I'm paralysed with fear. I know what a check-up means – an Aids test, and there's no way I'm having that. My parents are just being overly cautious because of Elsie. But I'm not Elsie.

Besides, if I am HIV-positive, I don't want to know about it. Why spoil a full, happy life with such ghastly knowledge? If I'm not sick, then what does it matter? I may as well enjoy the time I have and deal with what I need to, if it ever comes to that.

The following day, I am working out at the gym. After I shower, I decide to slip onto the scale and put my parents' minds at ease. Somehow, somewhere, I have misplaced ten kilos. My weight has dropped from seventy-four to sixty-five. Hey, that's not all that much, I assure myself, but hey, driving home I am deeply disturbed.

I wrestle endlessly with these thoughts over the following week. I have it. I'm sure I have it. I've had unsafe sex – of course I have it. Or maybe I don't. I'm not showing any symptoms. I read about *one* guy in America whose body was immune to the virus. Perhaps I'm like him. Anyway, I'll be safe from now on, so what does it matter? I shove it out of my mind. If I don't think about it, it'll go away, right? But it doesn't. And, privately, some very frightening thoughts continue to haunt me.

Over the next few weeks, my friends begin applying a little pressure. 'Are you sure you don't want to go for a check-up, Addie? Just to be safe?'

'I'll think about it.'

At one point, two of my dearest, Kate and Alex, invite me out for dinner at my favourite steakhouse. By mid-meal, it becomes evident that this is a sneaky set-up. They have brought me here to insist I take this situation in hand. It is an act of pure love, but I cannot see it. I feel tricked. Ambushed. I am furious. We gnaw uncomfortably through our steaks in the silence. More than ever, I am utterly resolved not to go for a test.

Only, the pressure doesn't ease – it increases. And so I begin to avoid the people who're applying it, until gradually it dawns on me that I am alienating the most precious people in my life. My feet are really aching at night now. It's that circulation thing, I figure. My GP gives me something to help ease the discomfort, but it's not very effective. One night, I awake on a pillow drenched with sweat. A night sweat! I've heard about Aids and night sweats, but hey, this is just a coincidence. So I lie there. The sweat dries, cold and sticky against my skin. I drive the fears out of my mind. There's some kind of explanation, I guess. Flu perhaps? Or nothing.

ENOUGH

23 July 2003

A WEEK LATER, I WAKE up wet again. Then, somehow, somewhere beneath a mountain of fear, I locate a tiny trickle of courage. I have run through the various possibilities in my head a thousand times now, like a hamster on some demented wheel, and I can take it no longer. My friends are beyond furious. I'm avoiding their calls. I've got to do it. It takes everything in me to make the terrifying, ten-minute journey to my doctor and face half a decade of denial. 'I think I might be HIV-positive,' I announce. 'I guess I'd better have an Aids test.'

The following day seems like a week. I can hardly believe I've done this. What trauma am I letting myself in for? I'm sure I'm positive. And so what if I am? I'll get some medicine and take it in hand and get on with my life. Thank God it's happened now. A few years ago, I'd have been dead. I'll probably never have a relationship again – who wants to be with someone who's sick – but who cares? I can deal with that.

Or, hey, maybe I will. I know of negative guys who're involved with positive guys. They just play it safe. Who knows? Maybe I'll find someone *because* I'm HIV-positive.

Maybe I'll hook up with someone cute in a support group. There are lots of cute guys who are positive. I've seen them in New York in their 'Poz' T-shirts. What the hell. I'm probably negative anyway, so now I can start from scratch. No more risks. A fresh start.

The following morning, I drive coolly to the doctor's office for the news. The meeting is brief and clinical. 'Yes,' he states matter-of-factly. 'Your tests came back positive, so you need to go and see a specialist, and you need to look for some kind of support group ... How do you feel about this? Are you okay?'

'Yeah, I'm fine. It's not really a surprise for me. I guess I've known for a while.'

I feel nothing. I don't ask if he's sure or if there just might be some mistake. This is a confirmation, not a revelation. I take the test papers and drive to my parents' office. I pace the room anxiously, waiting for both of them to be available. My voice cracks, and the words that come out of my mouth seem surreal. 'I've just been to the doctor. And I'm HIV-positive.'

I have no idea where it comes from, but suddenly we all melt down in tears. Dad hugs me and sobs on my shoulder. When did we last hug like this? This is what I've feared the most. The disappointment in my parents' eyes and the pain I'd cause them. They've offered me so many opportunities and I, in my carelessness, have brought this upon myself. I have failed them. What was I thinking, fucking without a condom? Of course I'm not immune to the virus. Of course I'm positive. I had the information and I ignored it. How could I have been so damn stupid?

If Mom and Dad are disappointed, they show none of it. Mom hugs me. Dad just keeps on crying. Little do I realise how close this disease will bring us in the following months. 'Whatever you need, don't worry about it,' Dad assures me. 'Financially, emotionally … We'll take care of it. We're with you, Boy.'

I didn't realise how incredibly lucky I was at that moment. How many parents would respond like this? There's no hint of judgement. No blame. No turfing me out of their lives. For so many people, this moment marks the opening of a vast rift, an onslaught of stigmas and embarrassment. So many parents can't deal with homosexuality, let alone with HIV. But since I came out to them, fifteen years earlier, my sexual orientation has felt increasingly natural around Mom and Dad. And one day, maybe this will too.

Who am I going to tell about this? No one needs to know, do they? My grandmothers certainly don't. They'll panic. They won't get it. And my cousins? No, not my cousins. And not my uncles and aunts. And what about the queens? Oh God! I can hear them bitching at the club already. *Oh, she deserves it! We saw her picking up guys and fucking around. Now she's Aida, doll! So thin! So uggh!* I tremble. *They* don't need to know. I owe them nothing. I'll tell the people who mean something to me. The people I love. And I'll do it now.

* * *

I drive home and dial Roy, Kate and Alex and ask them to come over. I don't give them any details on the phone. Just come over, I say.

They arrive separately within an hour. I break the news to each of them at the gate and usher them inside, where we all sit together on my big, deep, brown sofa. We're okay for a while, then one of us starts crying. Then all of us.

We brighten. 'It's such a relief to finally know,' I say bravely. 'At least now I can take control of it. I'll go to the doctor and get myself on anti-retrovirals and I'll live. They've come so far with HIV. It's not a death sentence any more. It's a manageable disease.' We smile. We hold hands. Then it's tears again.

Sure, there's hope, but no matter how much any one of us suspected this, its shocking confirmation tears us apart. So much surfaces this afternoon. The terror of pain and illness. The horror of mortality. I've let them down too, in a way. They are showing me so much love. I'm shocked at the extent of their sadness. I've numbed myself out for so long. I never imagined how shaky this would be.

After a few hours, I'm exhausted. I reassure them that I'm okay, see them off, and crawl into bed. My head explodes with fear. The gossip of bitchy queens babbles away like white noise in the background. My feet hurt. It's that damn circulation. I must get some sleep.

* * *

'Your cell counts are around 450 right now,' my GP announces. 'So there's no huge urgency. They'll usually only put you on the medication if you drop below 200. It's more important that you find the right person. Take your time.' I am relieved. This gives me some breathing space. I need to swallow the news slowly and digest it slowly. It still doesn't seem real.

But for Mom it did seem real. She's always been incredibly capable and giving, and by the next day it was clear she had made this her problem as much as mine. She began phoning around and calling me with feedback. *This* doctor was arrogant and unfriendly. *That* one couldn't give me an appointment for three months.

* * *

I don't remember the next couple of weeks very clearly. As my memory has it, I carried on with my life without any great changes. I worked for another week, but I'd begun to feel tired, so I stepped into my boss's office one afternoon to discuss it with her. Her response was sympathetic and generous. I'd better take a month of unpaid leave, I said. I just need to take this in hand, get on the medication, and I'll be back in September. 'That's absolutely fine,' she said. 'But I really don't see why your leave should be unpaid. It's not your fault you're ill. Take the time off and we'll see how it goes.'

I took it easy over the next few days, resting, reading, trying to make some sense of what was really happening to me. Or that's how I remember it, at least. My darling Kate remembers it differently. During that time, she says, 'You started losing it, mate.'

One morning, she came to my house with some flowers. She rang the doorbell and I didn't answer, she claims. She peered through the crack in the front gate and caught sight of me, lying on my bed, arm up, with a ciggie burning in my hand. She rang and rang but I didn't respond. She was devastated. I was losing my mind, she says. She went home in a state and called her husband in tears. I was finished, she said. Dementia had set in and I was going to go up in flames with my mattress. She couldn't reach me.

Mom and Dad were away for the weekend. Kate called and asked them to come home immediately. I remember the phone ringing that afternoon. I remember Mom recounting the story to me, but it made no sense. Kate hadn't been there. Or the bell wasn't working – only it was. I was fine. Kate was losing it. Or I was. Whatever. I'd see them the next day when they came home.

DR D

30 July 2003

A WEEK LATER, I FIND myself in the waiting room of Dr D's consultancy, flipping through *Men's Health*. Ten Steps to Killer Abs. Yeah right. I certainly won't be working out this month. Little do I realise, Kate has been so worried that she made an appointment for herself, so the doctor could offer her some explanation about what was happening to me. Wow!

She asked my mother to come with her and they showed Dr D my test results, but they made no sense to him. 'If his cell count is really 450, then why is he experiencing these symptoms?' he asked in alarm. He called the lab immediately and discovered a mistake, the dire consequences of which would only reveal themselves much later. 'Yes, his total cell count is 450, but his CD4 count (the number of white blood cells that make up his immune system) is already far lower than the 800 one finds in healthy people. It is also way below the magic 200 – below which medication is recommended.' Though I would only learn this much later, my CD4 count at that moment was a single digit.

Two.

'If you can get him here by one o'clock,' said Dr D, 'I'll see him today.'

* * *

And so Dr D runs me through a list of symptoms. They are all familiar to me – the very things I've been brushing aside as coincidences. Night sweats. Shivers. Diarrhoea. Pain in my feet. 'But that's just my circulation. Winter, right?' Dr D shakes his head gravely. 'It's a condition called neuropathy,' he explains. 'It affects 10 per cent of HIV patients, and up to a third of patients once they start taking anti-retrovirals. The virus damages the nervous system. You'll need to get on some painkillers.'

'Can you do something about it?' I ask.

'Unfortunately it's very difficult to treat. As for the HIV, I'd like to get you going on the anti-retrovirals as soon as possible.'

I have a cold, so we wait a week. The cold virus will make it difficult to accurately measure the levels of HIV in my blood. When it begins to clear the following week, I receive my first little selection of pills. The cocktail he chooses is a fairly common one, affordable and simple enough to adhere to. Three pills in the morning, three at night. Thank God, someone who knows what he's doing. This man found me just in time, I guess.

Besides his evident professionalism, there's something deeply reassuring about this young doctor. He seems sensitive, gentle, compassionate. Terrified as I am at the seriousness of the situation, I feel just a little safer driving home this afternoon.

The following day, Mom and Dad ask me to come and stay at their house. Predictably, I resist. 'Just for a week or two,' they say. 'Till you're over the worst.' Finally I agree, oblivious to what a week or two will become. This seems insane. I haven't lived at home since I was eighteen. I move into the guest suite – a combination of my old room and my sisters' rooms knocked together. It's far plusher and comfier than my house, though not quite my style.

It's big and beige. Beige walls. Beige curtains. Sisal carpeting. Some well-placed Chinese antiques set off against framed vintage prints. There are two comfortable cane wingbacks for guests. I feel like a guest, but I feel safe.

ANIMALS

5 August 2003

MY LIFE BEFORE I GOT ill was anything but ordinary. Before I departed for a two-year lifestyle experiment in New York, I'd made a rather outrageous name for myself on the Johannesburg party scene. If the outfits weren't enough to set tongues wagging, the behaviour certainly was.

In my late twenties I was part of a comfortable little gang. Alex and Kate were part of it, as was my friend Albert and his boyfriend, Jan. Various others became partners in the ongoing social crime spree, but we were the core. Together we were unstoppable – cruel occasionally, and often socially unacceptable. We wore one another's clothes and crashed at one another's homes. Whenever we were together, I felt invincible – beyond the stares of conservative onlookers, beyond the dismay of parents, chums or meeker acquaintances, beyond the law.

Costume was a constant player – the more shocking, the better. Drag is far too traditional a term for the sort of indescribable ensembles we dug out of the second-hand trunk. Sometimes there were drugs involved, sometimes they weren't necessary. Our combined energy was sufficient to initiate substantial public havoc.

Take a perfectly innocent dinner we arranged at our favourite restaurant, The Singing Fig. Albert had packed a little backpack of tricks for the occasion. The contents included a video camera, a couple of joints and a few bright silk sarongs I had recently bought in Indonesia. We got through the starters within our usual sedate behavioural bounds – napkins on the heads, a few impromptu monologues and a quiet joint passed surreptitiously under the table. By the second course, we were rocking. Albert had begun digging in the backpack. Soon enough the entire table of eight had been transformed into a shimmering tent. More joints were puffed beneath it and bursts of song and laughter rang through the restaurant.

I can only guess that the owners put up with all of this because we were a little less dull than the usual patrons. Perhaps we offended some people, perhaps we drew an audience. I know for sure that the waiters grew a little tired of it. Indeed, I recall, when everyone else had left, I was still crouched on all fours in the restaurant entrance, draped in a tablecloth, balancing a plate and some cutlery on my back and insisting I was Table Five. Drunk as I was, I do recall catching a glimpse out of the corner of my eye of the poor staff, all yawning patiently as I drew out my performance. Kate may have been laughing her head off, but after an eight-hour shift, I doubt *I'd* be in the mood for a late-night impersonation of Table Five.

COCKTAILS, ANYONE?

10 August 2003

TODAY, I BEGIN MY first course of Nevirapine – one of the earliest anti-retrovirals. I also start taking Triptelene, an anti-depressant that is known to bring some relief to neuropathy sufferers. I've been warned that there might be side effects, as my body rejects or accepts these drugs. Within a couple of days, I feel quite awful. Nauseous and unable to eat, I lie withering on my bed for days. One night, I wake up and need to pee. I stand up and the room begins to spin. I tumble flat on my face, smashing my head on a wooden cabinet. I try to get up, but I can't move. I am stuck and terrified. I yell for help.

Shocked, Mom and Dad lift me onto my bed. Dad lets me lean on his shoulders while I stagger precariously to the bathroom. I have lost so much weight I have little strength. I feel so helpless and humiliated. 'Just a dizzy spell. I'm sure I'll be okay.' Reluctantly, they leave me to sleep.

But the following morning it happens again. I make it further across the room this time, but before I can get to the bathroom, I tumble tragically again, against a red Chinese wedding cabinet. Slowly, I pick myself up and crawl to my bed. Where the fuck is my sense of balance?

The next morning, Alex comes to visit. She sits in calm horror at the edge of my bed. I feel ashamed to be seen like this, but I can't fake any strength. Mom brings me some food. It has no appeal, but I force some down in desperation. Within minutes I feel it surging up my throat. I puke. Mom calls the doctor.

'We're taking you to hospital for a little while,' she announces. 'We need to get you onto a drip so you have something going into your body.'

'I'll be okay,' I protest as usual. 'This will pass.'

'It's only for a day or two,' she pleads. 'The doctor really thinks it's the best thing, right now.'

'Come on Addie,' says Alex. 'We're taking you there.'

I have little choice but to accept.

* * *

Who likes a hospital? From the moment they wheel me through the sliding doors at the entrance, I can smell the sickness in the air. The creaking steel beds. The sloppy piles of food in old stainless steel containers. The germs dancing wildly, like it's *Saturday Night Fever*. The sick people, strangled in tubes. The bleeping machines. I hate this.

I've been promised a private ward, but it doesn't happen. The nurses prop me up on the bed so I can watch the television. A few friends arrive. There are bright flowers all around me. With the drip in place, I feel a little better. I need to pee, but I can't make it there myself. Dad and Roy carry me to the bathroom, drip intact. I'm so frail, I feel I could snap at any moment. My skin is pale grey. Later, Roy confesses how very frightening that moment was for him. 'Like an eighty-year-old man,' he says. 'Right then, I was sure it was over.' Everyone was, I guess. Except me.

The following morning, I wait hours for the doctor to arrive, but he doesn't. 'He'll come, he's very busy.' Eventually, when he does arrive, he decides to take me off the medication temporarily. The bad news is: My system is not responding positively to the anti-retrovirals. The dizziness is a rare side effect called ataxia, an extreme loss of balance, which may have been caused by the Triptelene. The good news is I can go home.

* * *

I struggle to recall the details of the next couple of weeks. Half the time I'm drowsy or asleep. I know it's mid-August and I know I was diagnosed at the end of July. So much has happened in these couple of weeks. Who'd have dreamt I'd be feeling so dreadfully sick so soon? Who'd have dreamt it would be like this? Aren't I just supposed to down the cocktail and carry on living my life? What the hell is going on?

Later that night, Dr D comes over and takes some blood. The following day, I learn that the cocktail is having a dangerous effect on my liver and that we'll have to change it. My parents write to someone they know in London who works in HIV. He recommends a combination of two new drugs. Dr D is quite happy with the recommendation, and so I commence my twice daily intake of Kaletra and Invirase. Together, these amount to sixteen pills a day, plus all the other bits and pieces I am taking. Depending on my ailments, the total will soon rise to anywhere between thirty-five and sixty highly toxic capsules into my body daily. Ouch.

* * *

Anti-retrovirals cannot destroy the HI virus. They can only prevent it from replicating. While some drugs attack the proteins of the virus, others destroy the protease that allows the virus to bind together and thus render it useless. Some new drugs block the entrance to the cells where the virus reproduces. Doctors use multiple drugs to ensure as powerful a fight as possible against the virus. Gradually some of the old virus dies and you start feeling better. At this stage your immune system can start building, but until it rises to the random-sounding but magical 200, you are vulnerable to a myriad of opportunistic diseases. I have no idea what these are, but they sound pretty scary.

And yet, each of our bodies is different. While one cocktail may work for someone, it won't work for someone else – either that, or its side effects prove so dangerous that it must be discontinued. Adherence to the drugs is critical. They must be taken at the same time every day. This is so strict that if you travel across time zones, you will need to wake up at some ungodly hour to maintain the schedule. If enough doses are skipped, you can build up a resistance to the drugs and they'll never work again. Eventually, new drug-resistant strains of the virus are created and some people become untreatable.

Unfortunately, even if one does adhere to the drugs, the body can still develop resistance and they will need to be altered. And there are only so many options. You run out of options, you die.

The extent of the virus in one's body is measured by a viral load test. One looks at the amount of 'copies' per millilitre of blood. Below 50 copies, the virus is undetectable. But the virus reproduces quickly. The 'copy' count can climb into the millions. At the time I begin treatment, my viral load is 429 000, which, I must point out, has never been a lucky number for me.

Once you're infected, the virus stays in your body. The trick lies in keeping it under control forever. These drugs can't save your life, but they can prolong it. But then again, what is 'saving a life'? Living for eternity? We can all but prolong our lives. According to some hopeful information I read, people with HIV on medication are likely to survive just as long as anyone else.

But do I want to?

WHORING

27 August 2003

THERE IS SOMETHING MYSTERIOUS and unexplainable about promiscuity. Right now, it seems the most remote reality to me. The thought of having sex with anyone, having a lover or even just making suggestive eye contact feels utterly alien. And yet for years it has been constant in my thoughts. It's a *man* thing, my girl friends tell me.

Since I broke my virginity a century ago, I have wrestled with this monster. Increasingly, as I grew older, I got into a pattern of seeking out men for one-night stands, having some quick fun and then berating myself with guilt for days afterwards. I've had a few serious, very loving relationships but this was something completely different. It crept up on me at times like an insatiable hunger – less of an expression of love or even lust, and more a desire to conquer beauty or power, own it briefly and then distance myself totally from it. There was always something thrilling about meet-ing a stranger, dicing a daring short cut through the standard protracted courtship rituals, and leaping instantly into intimate territories. It seemed so haphazard – as if it confirmed some weird belief in a delightfully random universe – as if my true love was waiting around the next corner. Only he very rarely was.

The monster tormented me. I had spent thousands in psychologist's bills discussing it over the years. I had acknowledged its dangers – both physical and emotional – and I had resolved to change my ways, but it was no good. While I was involved in relationships I behaved like a good little girl, but no sooner was I on my own, I'd be struck by a deep loneliness that sent me hunting in all the wrong places and landing up with all the wrong men.

Gay bars were the ultimate danger zones for me. Often I'd step out alone, in my sexiest possible get-up, and spend a few hours drinking Castle lagers, to horrible music. I'd scan the room for someone attractive. By the time I found him, my judgement was usually as slurred as my speech, and I'd embark on a conversation that would have had me cringing in the daylight. There'd be the usual trite compliments. 'You're a sexy guy, you know?' Some nauseating horoscope enquiries. 'Um, Capricorn, but I don't really believe in it.' Then a sad, ironic résumé of past relationships – as if these had anything to do with what was hotting up. 'Oh, so it didn't work out? D'you miss him? Are you looking for a relationship? ... Yeah, the *right* person ... I know what you mean.'

By the second drink, we'd be onto the inevitable career quiz. 'Oh, insurance? D'you find it interesting?'

Actually, at one point I resolved not to do insurance guys. I'd find some way of disappearing in a hurry. I just had to draw the line at insurance. It was just one of the trivial little games I'd begun playing in my dangerous and trivial pursuits.

There was something profoundly schizophrenic about this process. I became another person when I was in this mode. Intellectual snob that I am, there's no way I could have tolerated such facile conversation if I wasn't drunk. Most of the time, these were not the kind of guys I would dream of hanging out with. Beyond physicality, there was nothing that attracted me to them. And occasionally, when I did connect with someone, it would mysteriously fizzle to nothing. Embarrassed by the tacky circumstances of our introduction, we'd disappear shamefully after baring everything.

Of course, there was always a chance this would lead somewhere. A chance they'd call me or I'd call them and we'd become soul mates forever, but this didn't happen. On some level, I guess, I jinxed the encounters before they even began. I wanted the anonymity – some brief, forgettable intimacy before the next empty, meaningless conquest.

The upside of this was that, most of the time, the physical contact was not very intimate. There was rarely any actual sex, just some lies, followed by groaning and mutual masturbation. I didn't want to get intimate. Sometimes, I couldn't even bear the thought of kissing them. Oral sex was fine, but how could you kiss a stranger?

And so, most of the time, these encounters were physically safe. There was rarely an exchange of phone numbers – let alone bodily fluids. Often, once the excitement of stripping down and getting hard was done with, it was simply a case of getting it over with in a hurry. It was not that I didn't believe in romance. When sanity dawned, I knew there was nothing better than sharing a candle-lit bath with someone or telling stories all night, but somehow I managed to keep my carnal adventures in a totally different category.

Promiscuity fitted in well with my broader process of

denial, I guess. I was selective in how much I told my friends. If a guy was especially cute or we'd connected well, I might tell a friend about it. 'Hot, yeah. Who knows? Well, maybe …' But often I'd keep it secret. We'd meet at some godforsaken hour in some dingy club, have our fun and make sure there was no trace of anything by morning, and so it was easy enough to erase the whole incident from memory – though evidently not from other cells in my body. I'd wrestle with guilt for a few hours and then forget about it. Happily, these encounters came with an unspoken rule – if we happened to run into each other, a quick embarrassed nod of recognition – and sometimes not even that – was all that was required.

For a while, I found myself addicted to the gay chatlines. This was even more absurd. At the oddest times of day, I'd dial up and sit on my ass, flicking through the list of euphemistic nicknames. Bigdick. JoburgHunk. SexNow. I was pretty damn sure that Pretoria17 was really decrepit, and sixty-seven, but I continued with the dumb charade regardless.

'Stats?' was the standard opener. Six foot. Brown hair. Green eyes. Chest hair. Cut. Gym daily. Next up, 'Do you want to exchange pics?' Yeah, sure. And within seconds my desktop would be furnished with some anonymous image, stolen, no doubt, from a porno site. Sometimes, the photo was actually authentic. Good lighting and a decent crop worked wonders on the Net. My photo was real, but unfortunately all I had on my computer was a corny birthday shot with some arbitrary straight friends gathered around a table. It probably scared off quite a few guys, but what did it matter? For the most part, I didn't have the slightest intention of actually meeting for coffee. I'd just ring up a scary phone bill for an hour and then log off.

The few times I actually did agree to a meeting were disappointments. Of course, the hunks in question looked nothing like their photographs, and I'd find myself wondering what on earth I was doing, hiding in the corner of some arbitrary coffee shop talking about nothing in particular to no one of any consequence. In a year of cyberspace, none of this amounted to any actual sex. After the whole dumb rigmarole, I simply lost my nerve.

And yet somehow, in the gay community, this was considered normal. 'Doll, those boring chatlines,' we'd admit, and then hurry back to them. 'Oh! You got laid. I'm happy for you.' The bars, the clubs and the one-night stands were all considered part of a culture, and it was ours. For all the rejection we'd suffered, we were entitled to our own mysterious ways, and we weren't accountable to anyone about them. We faggots didn't want to come out of the closet – it was dark and exciting in there. Private and kinky.

Because the gay scene had its own history of secrecy and denial, it facilitated these sorts of encounters. Straight married men would do it. Gay men involved in relationships would sneak out and do it. And within the scene there was a weird kind of heroism attached to it. 'You scored, you bitch!' At the very worst, there'd be a trivial slap on the wrist. 'Oh, naughty girl, you'd better behave yourself!'

And so, generally, there was little catharsis in discussing

this with my gay friends. Only the occasional chat with my real girl friends would put me in touch with how ridiculous it was. Every now and then, I'd break down and fess up to Kate or Alex. We'd work through my guilt and I'd resolve to make some changes. It would work for a while, and then the cycle would commence again. The bars, the clubs, the Internet – on some level, I'd reduced it all to a game. I'd ration the opportunities. Okay, I've been out twice this week, I'll give it a break. And whenever I went home without meeting anyone, I felt like a failure.

Sometimes, I'd come across a quiz in some crappy women's magazine about how many people you'd slept with. I had no idea. In my now twisted memory, my past partners were faceless, nameless. Yet ask me how many people had really meant anything to me, and I could count them on one hand.

Deep down, I acknowledged how dangerous this lifestyle was for me emotionally. I realised that with each meaningless encounter, I was building more emotional walls around myself. The more times I faked closeness, the more unlikely a candidate I became for genuine intimacy.

It must be almost impossible for, say, a loving, monogamous heterosexual couple to make sense of this behaviour. From the outside it must seem filthy, decadent, even desperate, but, from the inside, it is an all-consuming hunger that gobbles you up. Over the past few months, my sex drive has plummeted. I have no interest in any physical intimacy. I am never horny. I guess, subconsciously, I've needed to demonise sex in some way, in order to heal. It is, after all, what made me so very sick.

When I happen to spot a porno in progress on a screen in a bar somewhere, I feel utterly nauseated – no arousal, no desire. The whole fucking culture seems stupid and dirty. Am I turning into some neo-puritan prude? Well, if I am, I'm fine with it. I guess my sins require some repentance – if they were sins. I'm not sure.

For a long time, I'd suspected the punishment for these crimes was death. That Aids was the final reckoning for this kind of behaviour. But this was not my own voice. We are all vulnerable to mistakes and failings. Many of us have vices or obsessions that we cannot control, and we must treat these not as crimes, but as illnesses that we are capable of managing. My psychological illness had now revealed itself in a tormenting physical one, and the healing of both of these was equally important.

I remember asking myself a few months before I got ill, 'If you could no longer have sex, would life be worth living?' The answer was a definite 'No'. I couldn't picture life without the regular ecstasy of an orgasm. But right now, I've shifted completely. If I don't get an erection for the rest of my life, I'll be quite fine with that. Perhaps it's because I am so sick right now. Or perhaps I'm healing.

BLAME

3 September 2003

AS I WRESTLED WITH THESE thoughts, my friends began asking me some obvious and unavoidable questions. 'Do you know when you got infected?'

'No. It could have been a few months ago, but

somehow I think it's been a while. I don't know for sure, but I sense it.'

'Do you know who gave it to you?'

'Really, I haven't got a clue. There are various times it could have happened. It doesn't matter.'

'Aren't you angry?'

'No. I'm not interested in seeking revenge on anyone. It was my responsibility to protect myself and I didn't. It doesn't matter,' I repeated. 'I guess what frightens me more is the thought that I could have infected other people.'

Oh God! To be responsible for anyone else's suffering or death! And yet, if I infected anyone, I did so unknowingly – or unsuspectingly at least. But then again, wasn't denial as much of a crime as intent? Well, fuck it. Either way, protection was their responsibility as much as mine.

There is nothing useful about blame. It dispenses with accountability and clouds everything. This had happened to me and I had allowed it to. And now, my only salvation lay in taking full responsibility for it all. I was shifting from a point of denial towards one of total awareness and ownership, and that alone afforded me a deep sense of relief.

Until recently, I have never felt totally comfortable with myself. No matter what I achieved, or how happy I was, there was always something niggling at me in the back of my mind. No matter how brave or good I was, at times, deep down, I had been a coward and this had compromised me immensely. I could write or counsel my friends with great depth and integrity and yet, all the time, I was lying to myself. The energy that it took to keep those lies buried has worn away at me over the years. And now, for all the discomfort and fear I am experiencing, I feel free. For the first time in years, I can face my reflection with total honesty.

BLIND SALVATION
29 September 2003

After a few weeks on my new cocktail, I was delighted not to be showing any life-threatening side effects. It appeared we had found the winning combination, though it sure didn't feel like it. Many days, I was too weak to get out of bed. If visitors came, I could barely prop my head up on the pillow. I spoke to the ceiling and hoped we knew each other well enough to dispense with eye contact.

I had known this for a while, but now it was about to happen – dearest Kate was relocating to Cape Town. She felt torn about leaving me and yet felt it was the best thing for her six-month-old baby. The thought of life without her frightened me. She had been a tremendous support. Besides, my circle of friends had already begun to shrink. Some people had initially shown concern and then lost interest. Others had vanished completely, unable to face illness or mortality. Even some of my parents' friends had severed ties. Fair enough, some people were so immersed in their own psychoses that the thought of anyone else's trauma seemed unbearable. But still, such cowardly disappointments had hurt us.

Already, some days were interminable. My few remaining close friends and my family were angels, but they had other commitments, and so, much of the time, I was on my own. And lying there, staring into space, I began to face the fact that my life had changed radically and would never be quite the same again.

For starters, I was thirty-four years old and living with Mom and Dad. Initially, a week had seemed too awful to contemplate, and yet here I was, months later, with little hope of returning home any time soon. I couldn't drive. Even if I could bear the pain of it, my feet were so numbed from the painkillers I couldn't tell one pedal from another. I'd checked out a neuropathy website. The first innocuous request on the site ran as follows: Would You Like to Donate Your Car? How encouraging, I thought. I read no further.

Unquestionably, my condition demanded a great deal of effort on my parents' part. I could do very little for myself and I had become a burden. I felt awful being so dependent on them, but there was little I could do about it. I had become a child again – or an octogenarian already.

Before this happened, I had taken so much for granted. Walking, eating, exercising, going out. I had lost all that, but above all I had lost my independence. I'd left home at eighteen and never looked back. I'd travelled all over the world, spending time in Cape Town, New York, Brazil, Zanzibar, Mali, Morocco and a hundred other incredible places, and now here I was, back at square one, in the very room I'd grown up in more than thirty years ago.

Dr D suggested I go and see a psychologist, but even this required Mom or Dad driving me there and waiting an hour in the car while I thrashed out my issues. Still, I thought it was a good idea. I'd had seven years of therapy in my twenties, but this was different. I had no intention of delving into my past, but I needed to make sense of my present.

The first sessions were helpful. We discussed the importance of keeping my mind alive. My health had improved marginally, but not enough for me to achieve very much. I needed to negotiate the line between sickness and wellness. I could do a little more now, and if I didn't make some effort, I would simply feel frustrated, and decline. But if I tried to do too much, I'd feel defeated. I should try to write or draw, he suggested – create something, express how I was feeling about what I was going through. After all, there was only so much satellite one could stomach without *boring* oneself to death.

I resolved to start getting well. Even if this was beyond my control physically, I could still play some part in my psychological recovery. I tried to write, but came up with very little. I felt very lost.

The newspaper was incredibly generous to me. A couple of times I had called and asked them to take me off the payroll. This was all taking far longer than I'd imagined and I felt guilty receiving a salary while I lay in my bed. But they had kindly refused. And so there was little choice – I would need to start coming up with some stories. Surely it was a mercy that I had chosen this career. As long as I could sit up, I could write, but just how I could write current affairs features when I had seen little beyond the four walls of my parents' guest room for the past few months, I wasn't sure. I racked my brain and came up with nothing. And so I lay around for September and

October, staring into space, waiting for visitors. And, sadly, when they arrived, I rarely had the energy to connect with them.

During one session at the shrink, we spoke about fear. 'What are you most afraid of?' he asked. 'Dying or suffering?'

'Well, suffering, I suppose. If I die, I'm done and I won't have to deal with it.'

'Have you thought you were going to die at any point?'

I pondered. 'No. Never.'

In that answer, I began to grasp what I would call my Blind Salvation. A trait, I realised, that was both a blessing and a curse. A curse – in that it had kept me in denial for so long. Convinced that I would never get ill, I had taken countless risks and left my diagnosis far too late. And I'd got much sicker in the process. But a blessing as well – in that, no matter how gloomy the signs were, never once had I pictured myself dying. Everyone around me had, but they'd never dared express it. And so, ironically, while my Blind Salvation had almost killed me, it was also keeping me alive.

DOPE MOM

1 October 2003

BEFORE I GOT ILL, I'd been a pretty dedicated marijuana smoker. I'd spend hours listening to music and drifting into space and thought. I adored the escape into romantic reverie. The escape from mundane sobriety.

Sometimes it helped me with my writing; sometimes it just helped me giggle with my friends. Often, we'd dress up and amuse one another with those little acts. Weak as I was now, I still managed to smoke.

I discussed the dope situation with Dr D, who said it was good for pain relief and nausea. Problem was, at this stage I was running out of stash. Soldier that she is, my dear mother took it upon herself to acquire the doctor's prescription. She had no idea where to begin. She called my friends. 'Hi. You won't believe this, but I need to buy some pot!' – a word straight out of the sixties. It became a running joke among all of us: Mom – the drug dealer! But she managed to help me score. Sometimes, if I was too weak, she even helped me roll a joint. She just hoped she wouldn't find herself scoring on some dodgy street corner.

Undoubtedly, we'd come a long way, baby.

A LITTLE PURPLE PILL

3 October 2003

ALTHOUGH THE DOPE HELPED a little, the pain in my feet had become a nightmare. I struggled to get shoes on my feet, and walking – even standing – was difficult. I'd heard neuropathy described as a 'kind of pins and needles', but this was closer to walking on a bed of nails. The pain was fierce and 24/7. Only high doses of codeine phosphate made it even vaguely bearable. The most merciful position was on my back, with my feet stretched out. Next best – on my side, with a pillow between my skinny knees. I alternated every hour or so, like a roasting chicken.

I spoke to D about this. Since the Triptelene incident, I'd been hesitant to try any further medical options. I had spent two weeks forcing down a supposed miracle cure – one whole lemon, liquidised, skin and all, with a glass of olive oil and a glass of orange juice. It was vile, and after a fortnight of this, twice daily with no results, I'd abandoned it. But I was ready to try something else. Dr D prescribed me a course of Neurontin.

A few days later, my feet seemed to be getting worse. The pain was excruciating. Also, it had begun shooting up my legs. There were new areas of pain. Muscle pain, I thought. I reported to Dr D, who said I should come off the drug. In rare cases, instead of helping the nerves, it could start eating into the muscles, but he wasn't convinced. As for the pain, I would need to switch to a stronger painkiller. I flinched when he said it. Morphine.

It came in the form of a very expensive little purple pill called MST. But, whatever they'd named it, it is an opiate, and essentially not very different from the heroin one sees junkies spiking into a last available vein in their crotches. But I was told this would offer me no hazed-out bliss, simply pain relief. And no matter how drastic this seemed, it did offer me some respite. I'd heard of morphine addiction, but D assured me this was okay. There was a difference between recreational drug addiction and pain relief. And so I began washing down the little purple pills – first just a few a day, and gradually a couple more. And a couple more.

CONTAMINATION

5 October 2003

SEEING THE SHRINK WAS helpful. We looked for practical ways to cope with the current mental and physical crises. I raised my fears about the gay community. Sadly, as he pointed out, there were some people who would not show much compassion and might scorn me. 'There are some weird attitudes around – almost contamination by association,' he explained. 'Some people won't want to be seen with you in case it makes them look sick too.'

Ridiculous as it sounded, it rang of truth. In a culture so obsessed with physical beauty, frailness, skinniness and bulging eyes were the enemy. While a handful of gay people were very active in Aids politics, generally, unless it had affected them, they wanted little to do with it. Unlike New York or London, here one very rarely saw sick people at the bars or clubs. Once they became visibly ill, they would simply disappear.

Of course, this was part of the broader picture of denial. If Aids didn't exist, there was nothing to be frightened of. You didn't need to wear condoms or minimise your sexual partners. If you couldn't see it, it wasn't there.

SOUTH AFRICA

15 October 2003

IT WAS CREEPY. LIVING IN South Africa, I had grown used to the images I'd seen on TV – emaciated black people, dying alone of Aids in dark, forgotten huts in the countryside. Shivering under threadbare blankets with huge hollow eyes. I knew the horrifying statistics. Four to five million South Africans were HIV-positive. Eight hundred people were dying of Aids each day. The highest number of infected individuals in the world. I knew all this as well as anyone else who followed the news. Only now I was part of that statistic.

I struggled to make sense of this. Now, when I switched on the TV, I yearned to feel some solidarity with these people. They were my brothers and sisters in this disease. Were they also struggling to keep their food down? I wondered. Did they also have sore feet? Where did they get painkillers? And how could they live without them? Were they having the same thoughts as I was? Had they struggled with promiscuity? Were they still in denial? Or were they enjoying a new freedom?

Now, when I read some frighteningly destitute story in the newspaper, I searched for a sense of empathy, but I could not access it. Sympathy, yes – but, somehow, these people seemed as distant and unimaginable to me as they ever had. Sure we were all suffering from the same disease. While my friends and family could never really understand the pain and fear I was experiencing, perhaps these *people in the papers* were grappling with the same horrors. I hoped for some kind of shift or revelation, but it never came.

Of course, this was natural. While we might have shared a disease, we shared nothing else. There was no way I could ever feel a true sense of empathy with these people, because of one crucial factor – money.

From the start, my parents were beyond helpful in this regard. They never asked me for a cent for doctor's visits or medication. They never even showed me a bill. Their discreet generosity was astounding. Given everything I was going through, they said, finances were the last thing I should worry about.

But for the people I saw on TV, money was everything. Without money, they had little hope in fighting this disease. How would they ever be able to afford anti-retrovirals? Or painkillers? Many of them couldn't even afford food. And so they were simply wasting away and dying. If I, with every available resource, was suffering so much, I could scarcely imagine what they were going through.

But money was not the only thing that was saving my life. With my body so weak, I was in desperate need of care and support. From the moment I became ill, my parents were the most wonderful caregivers. Tirelessly, they would attend to my needs and suffer my moods. Friends, too, made time to come and see me. They cried when I cried and they showed me all their love. Never did I sense the slightest sense of judgement from anyone around me. No one ever said 'You deserve this', or 'It serves you right.'

At this time, the South African government was dithering over whether or not to provide free anti-retrovirals to its dying people. There were all sorts of excuses. The health system was a shambles, and without the right systems in place, there was no way the drugs could be correctly administered and monitored. Judging by TB statistics, South Africans had a rather bad track record in adhering to drug routines. And this meant their bodies could develop a resistance to the drugs.

If those with resistant strains continued having unsafe sex, we would be left with huge numbers of untreatable cases.

And there were other obstacles. Our country's president, Thabo Mbeki, had elicited worldwide controversy when he seemed to suggest that he did not believe that HIV caused Aids. He had stumbled across this information on the Internet, apparently, and it was contrary to any medical views. With the cause of Aids in doubt, the need for anti-retrovirals was debatable.

The Health Minister, Manto Tshabalala-Msimang, was not much more help. According to her, nutrition was the key to fighting the virus. She prescribed various herbal cures, from the African potato to a diet of lemon, garlic and olive oil, which was said to do wonders for the immune system. Meanwhile, the critical crusade for available drugs lagged tragically behind. Given the number of deaths, the government's slow negligence in supplying the necessary medication seemed to some of its critics to amount to nothing less than genocide. And I was inclined to agree with them.

Though few realised, the bureaucratic rot had actually set in long before this country's transition to democracy. Before Aids was a 'black' disease, it had been a 'gay' disease, and the deep-rooted homophobia of the apartheid regime had stymied all efforts to acknowledge and address the disease during the critical period of the late eighties and early nineties. Despite the internationally applauded miracle of the new South Africa, with regards to the survival of its people, the prejudices of one government had simply made way for another's. With such a legacy of denial to gloat over, the severity of South Africa's Aids crisis was hardly surprising.

I knew a couple of other people who were HIV-positive. I knew of people who'd died of Aids, but it had never been anyone I was close to. I had never watched anyone suffering, and for all the statistics I'd been bombarded with, I'd had no idea what Aids was really like. I'd been so convinced that with modern medical advances I would simply pop a cocktail and continue to live a normal life that it had never occurred to me how much pain and illness was involved. No one around me had any clue either. Perhaps I should publish all my scribblings someday, I figured. Perhaps, in some tiny way, it could be useful.

* * *

Since the first weeks of my illness, I had been capturing my experiences on my laptop. I made entries every couple of days, but I made them for myself. For as long as I could remember, writing has been my solace. I have always been driven by an instinctive urge to record the significant, often bewildering, events of my life, and, generally, writing has proved the best way I can make sense of them.

I played with the idea of publishing this memoir someday, but I knew that would entail a frightening degree of public exposure. As the weeks passed, I grew more comfortable with friends and family knowing about my illness. Despite my initial reservations, by that stage my entire extended family knew about it. Keeping it a secret had been impractical, almost impossible. My illness had become a full-time job for my parents and they'd needed to explain it to those around them. Only my grandmothers were spared.

Family was one thing, but coming out about this to the nation? I'd never get a date again – that was certain. What was I to become – the pitiful public face of Aids? I thought deeply about this. Rationally, there was no one I was beyond telling. Given the stigmas associated with Aids, I felt compelled to deal with my status with candour and honesty. But, emotionally, I wasn't ready to become some contaminated celebrity. Later, perhaps. Right then, the prospect overwhelmed me.

OCTOBER SURPRISE

10 October 2003

I'VE NEVER BEEN VERY good about going to the doctor. As with HIV, I've always ignored the littlest ailments, hoping they'd mysteriously disappear, and avoided them until they'd done some damage. Indeed, my negligence in getting tested had almost cost me my life. Dr D beseeched me not to ignore anything at this stage, to contact him with the slightest abnormalities. For the most part, I did so, and so I felt quite comfortable popping in for a check-up.

We talked a while, and then I remembered something. 'I have this little rash on my arm,' I said. 'Do you want to take a look?'

Dr D looked at it carefully, feeling it, switching on a bright light. He was silent. My left eye was also quite red, so he examined that too. 'Oh no,' he paled. He paced the room. 'I'm afraid it's what I thought it was. Kaposi's sarcoma.'

Dr D coolly explained that this was a type of cancer, often associated with HIV. 'With a decent immune system it might heal on its own,' he explained, 'but in your condition, I don't want to take any chances. I'm going to send you for a few blasts of chemotherapy.'

I was devastated. Aids *and* cancer? What was that about? How was my now withered system supposed to survive this? As with the almost devastating progression of the HI virus in my body, I was totally unprepared for the monsters waiting to attack me. This was not only due to the general silence around the disease that dare not speak its name; frankly, I'd been too frightened to research much. I took the oncologist's number and made an appointment for the following week.

During that time, I created a monster in my head. I knew nothing about chemotherapy, so I pictured myself being wheeled into tunnels and blasted with something nuclear. The day before the appointment, I lay on my bed, sobbing inconsolably, insisting that I wasn't going. I knew there was little point in this, but, as often lately, I was frightened.

The oncologist was very professional. He lacked the warmth I'd grown accustomed to with Dr D, but he sat us down and explained the various therapeutic options. There were three choices. The most expensive of these had a 75 per cent success rate and caused few side effects. The next offered 50 per cent's worth of hope. The last option was far cheaper but had a 25 per cent success rate. Side effects were inevitable. I was amazed. Little had I realised how much wealth had to do with this disease. Unjust as it seemed, cancer was for the rich. And the 75 per cent option was not just expensive. It was exorbitant.

I sat quietly, waiting for my father's response. He'd offered to foot the bill, so the ball was in his court. He paused. 'Well, I think we must go for the best course of action,' he said.

I was humbled. His generosity amazed me. I was being given a fighting chance simply because my parents could afford it. People in state hospitals often waited months for their treatments, getting sicker all the time. I was blessed. 'Well, okay then,' the doctor declared. 'Let's get going straight away.'

The chemotherapy ward was nothing like I'd pictured. The gloomy, surgical pit of my imagination was in fact a large, bright semicircular room, with French doors opening onto a pretty garden with a koi pond. Around its rim was a series of puffy armchairs, furnished with a group of cheerful-looking people with drips in their arms, flipping through magazines and chatting. The nurses were noisy and animated. It seemed more like a tea party than a cancer ward. For all the death that hovered in the background, the atmosphere was charged with life.

A nurse approached me with the said R20 000 bag of pink liquid. 'Time for your Red Bull,' she joked. I nestled into a chair and braced myself for what was to come.

'Pump up those veins,' she barked. She seemed bossy and boisterous, but when I told her how sensitive my feet were, she treated me with gentle compassion and respect. You go girl, I figured. In that case, be as boisterous as you like. 'Come on man, pomp!' she bossed, and then, very carefully, inserted a needle into a bulging vein. The Caelyx was cold – straight out of the fridge – and I felt a stiffness as it surged up my arm. She put a heated little beanbag over it to warm me up. This helped. But an hour and a half of this? Could I bear it?

The pain was not nearly as bad as I'd expected. I flipped through magazines and wolfed down a McDonald's yuckburger. McDonald's was next door to the cancer clinic, and over the following months a cheeseburger and apple pie were to become some sort of twisted tradition. Chemoburgers. The single cheeseburgers were the best, 'cos I could munch 'em with one hand. The other arm had the drip.

After an hour and a half, I was exhausted. Keeping my feet in one place all this time had left me sweating and irritable. Pale and dripping, I headed home and collapsed into bed.

I experienced no side effects during the next few days, but it had been traumatic. I slept a lot. At least I had a month until the next dose. I had coped with so much thus far. And I would cope with this.

JESUS DRAG
12 October 2003

THE LONG-HONOURED DRAG tradition in my circle of friends had produced a fine trunk of classics collected from charity stores over the years, and we were amply equipped with the indispensable tools of glitter, make-up and bad costume jewellery. Male or female, it didn't matter. It had nothing to do with perfecting the art of gender transform-ation, but everything to do with hauling out the drag trunk and digging out the most tasteless combination of frocks, wigs and objects of uncertain application, and then tangoing around the house with the music turned full-blast. Many people wouldn't have found it funny, but it was our private joke and I missed it.

A few nights after my first chemo session, while Alex was visiting, we got really stoned. My weight had dropped to around fifty-one kilos, my arms were sticks and my ribs were protruding like someone's I recalled from the Kosovo war coverage on TV. It wasn't that I hadn't eaten, but rather that my heavily medicated body was unable to absorb the food. I had been struggling to look at myself in the mirror, and usually I shut my eyes whenever I changed my shirt, but stoned as I was, I decided to take on my self-image. I stripped down, stretched out my arms, crucifix-like, and began parading around the bedroom, lip-synching to some Gregorian chants. 'Jesus Drag, Al! What d'you think?'

Alex shrieked, but she couldn't bear to look. The humour was a little bleak for her, she conceded.

I'd seen a film once, in which 'HIV Gals' in black bikinis and umbrellas floated down a river of blood, singing something tasteless. The image had stayed with me for years. 'But Aids is funny!' I protested. 'It makes you look funny, doesn't it?'

'Yeah, but there's a lot about Aids that isn't funny.'

'So does that mean I can't be funny any more? I can't be irreverent? Or ironic? Or does it just mean I can't be funny about Aids? Or can only I be funny about Aids because I have it, like Jews can make Jewish jokes? My God, if we can't find something funny in everything, then we might as well give up right now!'

I knew it was necessary to respect the sacredness of certain things, but sometimes that sacredness grew so intense, it began to paralyse me in fear and awkwardness. Aids had caused plenty of that already. And for someone in my condition, Jesus Drag seemed like a very good look. And so, over the following weeks, whichever poor soul happened to grace me with a visit, was treated to a star performance.

FIFTY-SIX

1 November 2003

A COUPLE OF WEEKS LATER, Dr D was ready to test my blood again. I shouldn't expect any miracles, he said, and I shouldn't be alarmed by the results. The healing took a long time. If my viral load had been 429 000, he hoped it had dropped to around 4 000 at this stage.

A week later, D called me with the results. His voice

was clearly emotional. 'I'm pretty blown away by this,' he said. 'Remember I said 4 000? Well, take a guess ...'

I couldn't.

'Okay. Right now, your viral load is 56! That's almost undetectable! I never hoped for such a drastic improvement.'

'And my CD4 count?'

'That takes much longer,' he said. 'It's risen from 2 to 6, but don't worry at all about that. What matters is that we have the virus under control and you can start to heal. Now, we just have to keep it there.'

My parents were overjoyed. Over the next few days, I heard my mother trying to explain the complicated statistics to everyone over the phone. We celebrated. I invited some friends round and I drank half a beer. I'd pretty much lost my taste for alcohol. With all the morphine I was taking, even the dope had little effect. It just gave me a headache and grogged me out. It was hilarious. For years, I had defied all authority and puffed away illicitly. Now, under doctor's orders and my mother's gracious collaboration, I had lost all interest.

GRANNY HELEN'S MIRACLE

5 November 2003

THE WEEKS PASSED AND I began to work a little. The newspaper gave me some books to review, and I felt greatly relieved to be producing something for them. I read voraciously. My own book, *The Wonder Safaris*, was finally being published and the launch was scheduled for 6 November. I was excited but anxious. I had waited so long for this auspicious event, only now I was so frail and ill, I was not sure I could handle it. I had scarcely left my bed for weeks. Now I was to face a crowd of a hundred people or more. Many of them had not seen me since I got sick. There would be surprised faces, no doubt, and questions and muttering, but so what? I no longer had anything to hide.

Mom helped with the planning. We had tried to fatten me up for the big night, but our hopes for a big scrumptious Christmas pig had been unsuccessful. It was painful being this skinny. Not only did I have little strength, but without any protective blubber I struggled to sit or even lie down at times. If I ever managed a visit to a restaurant, I would do so armed with an embarrassing pillow. Given my feet, bathing had also become a nightmare. Miraculously, Mom had hunted down a pair of wearable black velskoens, but most of the time I was condemned to a pair of unattractive blue slippers lined with a crusty layer of dried skin. Even fashion, it appeared, had deserted me.

As the big day drew closer, I received requests for interviews from magazines and radio stations. Most of these were on the phone and quite manageable, but the TV appearances were challenging. I was pale and thin and anaemic – not quite the picture of literary radiance I hoped to present to the world.

I did my best, covered up my blotchy skin with base and disguised my skeleton in baggy clothes. C'mon, be a soldier, I'd tell myself. The first TV interview went very well. I was obviously not in good health, but my energy and enthusiasm came across loud and clear.

For the past five years or so, my Granny Helen had been adamant that I was to write a book. It had become something of a joke: each time I saw her, she'd say, 'Where's that *book*? You'd better hurry up, my boy, I won't be around forever.' I had been so delighted when I could finally announce to her that I was being published, and had spent a few afternoons reading her extracts that had brought tears to her eyes.

A month or so before, my father had finally told her I had Aids. Although she was ninety-one, she was sound enough to handle the news without panicking. My maternal grandmother, we'd decided, would not be able to process the information, and so we'd kept her in bewildered ignorance with lame excuses and lies about a blood disease. I knew this was the best thing for her, and yet, somehow, I couldn't help feeling sick at the dishonesty. So much about Aids was a lie, and here I was – participating. I cringed at the thought of living in shame, but this wasn't about me. It was about sparing someone else some unnecessary trauma.

As the disease progressed, I felt stifled by the little lies surrounding it. How many people were coasting along on vague medical explanations, terrified to say the word 'Aids'? I asked Dr D about this at one point. 'Incidentally, am I HIV-positive or do I have Aids?' He confirmed the latter. There was something deeply hypocritical in all this, I realised. It was so much easier to say 'HIV-positive' – a common, manageable disease that posed no immediate life threat. 'Aids', on the other hand, was a word people didn't want to hear. Aids meant suffering, death and malnourished stick figures, abandoned in empty huts. The word frightened people. And from that point onwards, I resolved to challenge all this. If any explanation was required as to my appearance, I'd simply announce, as casually as possible, 'I've got Aids.' This would make it more real for me and help others become familiar with the reality that was invisibly surrounding them.

One morning I was shopping for comforts in a mall. My feet were sore, and I pressed the shop assistant quite aggressively to hurry with ringing up my goods. 'Oh, sorry dear, have you had an operation?' she asked. 'No,' I said. 'I've got Aids.' She was silent. The very sound of the word in a public place rang out eerily. She rang up the goods and smiled gently. 'I hope you feel better soon,' she said. So did I.

November 6th arrived, the day of the launch. Mid-afternoon, we received the news that Granny Helen had been admitted to hospital. There was some irregularity with her heart, and while she wasn't critical, the doctors wanted to monitor her. What cruel irony – after years of waiting and encouragement, she would ultimately not be able to attend my book launch.

Around 6 p.m., I made my way to the bookstore. It was a very special night. Friends had flown in from around the country and, scanning the room, I saw nothing but love. I sat at a table, signing copies of the book until my arm tired. The line seemed endless. I didn't recognise some of the people, and so I awkwardly left out 'Dear So and So' on their copies.

'It's Karen!'

'Oh, of course! I know it's Karen! How are you?'

By 8 p.m. I was exhausted. A dozen of us proceeded to a restaurant and enjoyed a memorable feast in celebration. The evening had been a triumph. My friends had made funny and heart-warming speeches and the book sold well. It was only later that some photographs confirmed how desperately ill I looked that night. In my blind salvation, that detail had totally eluded me.

Around 4 a.m. the following morning, my parents received a call from the hospital. Granny Helen's heart had given in and she had left us. There was great sadness among us, and yet there was no sense of a tragedy. She had lived a long, full, healthy life and had shared much love. Recently, she had told us she was ready to die. She didn't seem scared. She was happily resolved not to suffer or become a burden to anyone. She was quite satisfied with the life she'd lived.

My aunt had been at the launch, and afterwards she went to visit Granny, who was bright and alert and delighted to hear the details about the event. I was amazed at this woman's power. She had transcended the laws of mortality – simply choosing when she wanted to go and allowing it to happen. She had waited for this day for many years, and finally it had come. Miraculously, she had timed and willed her departure to a precise, appropriate moment. I hoped that one day I might simply disappear with such grace and dignity. Without anyone needing to say: 'Ag shame.'

TB OR NOT TB?

12 December 2003

OVER THE NEXT FEW weeks, the excitement of the launch died down. I was struggling with my health. Sometimes, in the late afternoons, I'd break into a horrible shiver. My entire body would shake, and my already sore feet would rattle on in agony. Eventually, after anything from thirty to sixty minutes under a couple of blankets, it would pass. My hands got the coldest, but my feet hurt the most. The trick was catching it as early as possible, or, better yet, anticipating it before it began, then bundling up and minimising the drama.

Inevitably, once my body was warmed up, I'd break into a horrible sweat. Then I'd have to swap the blankets for towels and mop up the streams as they poured from my scalp and temples. This usually took another half an hour, accompanied by a fever. The whole ordeal would usually last a good two hours. I complained to D about it, but he wasn't terribly worried. It was a good sign, really – it meant my immune system was starting to kick in, and though it was a damn nuisance, I'd just have to put up with it.

Gradually, I'd begun adapting to a new schedule. My feet were too sore in the evenings for me to do anything. The days were decent, but generally from 4 p.m. onwards I was confined to my bed until morning. Gradually, the reality of my curfew dawned on me. I had sacrificed so much freedom, and now I was to surrender my evenings as well. No late-night coffees with chums. No bar life.

No clubs. Nothing after dark. It frightened me. For so long, the nightlife had been my most prized distraction. I'd suffered through the dull weeknights only to party like crazy come weekend. But this, for now, was history. What's more, I couldn't travel long distances by car without feeling very ill. My world was definitely getting smaller. I could feel myself sinking into a depression. The beast of self-pity was lurking somewhere nearby.

A week later, I agreed to try out an acupuncturist for my feet. This involved stripping the socks off my swollen feet and facing them – something I'd tried to avoid. They were so sore most of the time, I was happiest not looking at them, touching them or even acknowledging they were there. God forbid anyone else touched them. They were so sensitive, if someone walked within a few centimetres of them I could sense it – like some kind of weird radar. I lived in terror of someone knocking them accidentally.

The acupuncturist gave me a tub of warm water for my feet and connected electrodes to my shins and behind my knees. The mild electric current was meant to stimulate circulation, perhaps even decrease the pain somewhat.

At this point, she'd insert some needles into my scalp and neck, more into my elbows and hands, and I'd sit there, all spiked and wired up, and break into a flood of sweat. It was hideous. I wasn't sure if it was the needles or simply that I was feeling ill generally. I managed two sessions and then decided to give it a break until I felt stronger.

I was anxious at the time. Mom and Dad had selflessly decided to have separate holidays so as not to leave me alone. ('D'you know what our biggest problem is?' Dad would confess later. '*Nothing* is too much of a sacrifice for us.') And so Dad was in Cape Town for ten days and Mom was set to leave on his return. This left me especially anxious. I had grown very dependent on her – for my meals, my pills, a response to my every bleat when I couldn't get out of bed.

We paid a visit to Dr D. I complained of various symptoms – the sweats, the nausea, the shivers. He examined me and then, sensitively as ever, he broke the news. 'I'm pretty sure what's happening here,' he said. 'I will do a test, but I'm so convinced, I'm going to put you on medication before I have the results. It's TB.'

I had known this was a likely possibility for people with such compromised immune systems, but I didn't realise how it would impact on me. 'Is it curable?' I asked. 'Absolutely,' he replied. I would require nine months of treatment and I could hope to start feeling better in a couple of weeks. In the car, on the way home, I called Dad with the news. As I said the word 'tuberculosis', I just burst into tears. Yes, it was curable. Yes, I was in the best possible hands. But, God, did I need this, on top of everything else? Just how much was my body expected to bear?

For centuries, TB had been a killer. It held notes of both tragedy and romance. I'd read tales of nineteenth-century aesthetes retiring to pleasant, Mediterranean climes to recover. But, right now, as the sweat dripped from my brow and my head ached, there was nothing romantic about it.

Mom postponed her trip. A week later, she left me in the kind hands of my father, who understandably was a little daunted by the temperamental dietary requirements and daily capsule regiments. But somehow Dad coped, and so did I.

HAPPY NEW YEAR
1 January 2004

IF I WAS GOING TO publish something about living with Aids, how was I going to write it? Since I'd begun toying with the idea, all sorts of people had pitched up with books by cancer survivors. I looked at them, but I couldn't bring myself to read them. Frankly, I couldn't think of anything worse than reading them. Now here I was, thinking of publishing something similar? What would it be? A list of my ailments? God knows, I could fill a few pages with those. But who'd want to read it? You know when you visit some ailing great-aunt and you enquire how she is and you wish you'd never asked. Was that the sort of protracted complaint I hoped to publish?

Something else worried me. I'd watched enough episodes of *Oprah* to familiarise myself with the nature of survival tales. As far as I could tell, these entailed: fessing up to Oprah, brushing away a tear, and resolving publicly to address your evil ways. The studio audience would applaud and the safe mediocrity of the world would be happily reaffirmed. Somehow, my predicament seemed a little more complex than this. Even if I survived, I could not quite picture myself playing that particular part of the redeemed survivor.

That evening, I spent a special New Year's Eve with my friends Ren and Teri. I was out until 1 a.m. – a triumph. I wondered why I'd spent so many years standing in line for some dumb club night, just to queue again, throw down a bucket of tequila and snog some stranger. It was so much more meaningful to celebrate with the ones I loved. To watch Ren dancing a jig in their living room. To defy my wretched curfew, glance at my watch and realise it was 1 a.m., 1 January 2004, was all I needed.

And so I was happy. I was also quite excited, as I had an appointment scheduled with the oncologist for that week. I'd made it through the prescribed cycle of chemotherapy and the prospect of a visit seemed quite routine. I'd have a biopsy, and the results would confirm the signs thus far – that the medicines had controlled the cancer to a point where my feeble immune system could take over.

And so Dad and I drove to the oncologist's office. As often at that time, I was struggling with the pain in my feet and I'd become quite short in my responses to people. Dad asked me about an article of mine that had been published that morning. 'Well, why don't you read it?' I snapped.

He was silent. 'I know you're in a lot of pain, Boy, and I'm sure it's hell, but do you have to be so short with me?'

I felt ashamed. He'd shown me nothing but kindness, patience and generosity, and this was his reward? How dare I? I apologised, and resolved not to make my pain anyone else's problem again. All around me, there were angels showering me with care: the least I could offer them was some courtesy and respect.

We arrived at the chirpy oncology clinic. I chatted a little with the doctor and he examined me. He then walked over to his desk and spoke gravely, without emotion. The news was not good. Despite the initially positive response to the treatment, the cancer had returned. The bruise on my upper arm was inflamed and my eye was redder. 'The treatment is obviously not effective,' he said. 'If the cancer is progressing while you are on treatment, there is little chance of recovery once you come off it. I could continue with this course, but, frankly, it might do little more than keep the advancement at bay and cost your parents an awful lot of money. I think we should try another drug.'

My heart sank. Just when I thought I was in the clear. If this first course had failed, what was the likelihood of a second one working? Could I bear another six months of needles and poison? I doubted it.

The doctor explained the new drug to me – Taxol. It was cheaper, but needed to be administered fortnightly instead of monthly. There was also the question of side effects. While these had been minimal on my previous course, now it was pretty much assured that I would suffer hair loss, nausea and a range of other discomforts. Most frighteningly, however, the drug was known to cause neuropathy. The pain in my feet was already unbearable. How could I possibly survive it getting worse? But 'unbearable', as I was to learn, is an extremely relative term.

The doctor assured me that any exacerbation was unlikely. The pain may even improve if the nerves die, he said. As for any other side effects, we would treat them as necessary. 'I think we should begin immediately,' he said.

'Pomp!' The nurse dug the needle into my arm. I was to receive a bagful of cortisone and anti-nausea medication, then wait twenty minutes. Then I could start the two-hour-long ordeal, watching the Taxol drip out of the glass bottle. The previous drug had been administered in an hour, sometimes forty minutes, but this procedure ran close to four hours. This was a test of resilience, I told myself. Not pain so much as discomfort and the horrible thought of this toxin being pumped into me. Stamina. Sitting in a single position for this long added strain to my feet. After four hours of watching the drip, drip, drip, I dragged myself to the car. I was devastated by the day's news and I was exhausted. I collapsed onto my bed in a river of sweat and tears.

DARKNESS

5 January 2004

THE WEEKS THAT FOLLOWED are the darkest in my memory. For the past six months I had lived on hope. Hope that – however slowly – the treatments would somehow work and my quality of life would improve. But now, all that had changed. For the first time in the whole frightening ordeal, I was finally convinced that I was going to die, and soon. I knew that cancer was a mercurial beast and a killer. And, lying in my bed, too weak to move, I spent the next week thinking the very worst.

A few days later, Roy and Alex came to visit. We chatted a little and then I broke down. 'I'm just not ready to go yet,' I sobbed. 'There are so many things I still want to do. Places I want to go. Ways I want to live.' We all cried, because it was real. There had been so many days I'd taken for granted, whiling away the afternoons smoking joints or writing meaningless stories. Although I'd never contemplated suicide, my mortality had never seemed this close. I'd been fatalistic about life. Whatever. When it happens, it happens. But right then, my will to survive was facing unprecedented challenges.

Faced with the terrifying prospect of spreading cancer, organ failure and consequent death, life seemed incredibly precious to me. As I lay on my bed, there were suddenly so many things I still wanted to achieve. People I wanted to meet. Books I wanted to write. And any apathy I'd indulged in the past suddenly made way for a burning desire to survive.

As I sobbed, I resorted to bargaining with someone who had previously been quite foreign to me – God. The words came gushing out with the tears. 'I know I've been a naughty boy,' I cried. 'I know I've been bad to myself and irresponsible and I probably deserve all this, and I'm ready to suffer for my sins, but I'm different now. For the past six months, aside from smoking these blasted ciggies, I've been a very good boy. I've taken my medicines. I've cut out drugs, sex and alcohol. I've been brave. I haven't complained. For the first time in my life, I've taken responsibility for everything. I've been good, good, good, and I promise, I'll be even better from now on. Oh please God! Can't you spare me? Can't you get me through this?'

I'd never been much of a taker for religion. I'd never really prayed, and the last time I stepped into a synagogue was at my bar mitzvah. Like my father, I was a committed and sometimes outspoken atheist. But now, faced with my mortality, I'd grown desperate. There seemed nowhere to turn but to a higher power. This outburst probably sounded ridiculously sentimental and out of character to my friends, but it was a sincere and desperate call. My fear was real. But, in time, the tears crumpled into laughter and Alex and Roy consoled me with flickers of hope. I felt better, but still utterly terrified.

* * *

I was scheduled to see Dr D the following day. Dad said he wanted to come with us. He was tired of hearing all the news second hand, he said. He felt excluded and asked to be present. I was unsure how I felt about this. His request was fair enough, and yet I experienced a sinking feeling in my gut. The very thought of the whole family arriving at the doctor's rooms for this consultation felt like the ceremonial making of my funeral arrangements – as though we'd all assembled to confront the very worst. I voiced my fear to Mom, but decided to put it aside. Dad's request was perfectly valid. After everything he'd done for me, how could I possibly refuse?

And so, the following morning, we made our bleak journey to Dr D's rooms. He suggested I see him on my own first. He examined me and sat down. He spoke gently and frankly as ever. 'I've got be honest with you,' he said. 'The situation is not good. Ironically, the reason you're getting sicker is because you're getting better. Your body is fighting the cancer and the cancer is fighting back, saying "Hey buddy. I'm not leaving. I'm staying put." Now, whether your body is *better* enough to get better, or too sick to pull through, really hangs in the balance at this stage. You need an immune system to fight the cancer, and yet the chemo is suppressing your immune system. It's a Catch 22.'

'Oh D.' My voice broke and I began to cry. 'I've been so frightened. I was so sure I was coming here today to talk about dying.'

He paused. 'This is not a good situation,' he repeated. 'But you don't come here to die. Here we deal with living. I'm not giving up on you. There are positives in the situation, and right now we're going to work with the positives.'

I thanked him and told him how anxious my parents were. He offered to meet with them afterwards and reassure them. His care, sensitivity and generosity were astounding.

THIRTY-FIVE

9 January 2004

THE FOLLOWING WEEKEND WAS my birthday. Although I was not in a celebratory mood, I was sure a get-together would lift my spirits. I invited ten people around for dinner. I helped my mother prepare a Thai curry and invent some strange, bright flower arrangements for the table.

I was pale and very frail. The new chemo drug had affected my blood levels and left me feeling very weak. I sat huddled in a sweater as my friends arrived with gifts.

The spirit was remarkable. A couple of surprise guests delighted me and everyone was in a great mood. We munched, posed for photographs, I even hobbled a little dance at one stage. The party continued until midnight. Despite my current state of fear, I felt surrounded by love that evening. It all seemed so normal that for a few moments I even forgot I was ill. I was thirty-five, and my life was hanging by a thread.

FROM MY BED
25 January 2004

SOON AFTERWARDS, I BEGAN work on a second book. Called *The Art of African Shopping*, it was intended as a guide for amateur art buyers, interspersed with anecdotal tales of my trips around the continent. The prospect daunted me. I could scarcely move from my bed. Travel was out of the question. I was convinced I'd published everything of interest in *The Wonder Safaris*. And while that book had been a compilation of years of work, this entailed starting from scratch, and I had no idea where to source new material. It seemed doomed somehow, but I'd been discussing it with my publisher for months. So I resolved to give it a bash.

My friends were amazed. 'You're writing another book in your condition?'

'Well, I'm trying to write another book. We'll see how it goes.'

I thought of the great Mexican artist, Frida Kahlo, and how much she had achieved and what a full life she had led, writhing in pain and confined to bed. Great intellectuals came to her bedside to stimulate her with conversation, and in a final triumph of individuality and defiance, she was carried into her exhibition opening on her bed, prettied up with flowers and those great Mexican peasant robes. It was a historic moment. Faced with severe limitations, she had sought out not normality, but excellence. For all the excruciating operations she'd suffered, she had resolved to transcend mediocrity. And if Frida could do it, so could I.

And so I set to work – squeezing out distant memories and writing about them in detail. I borrowed some of my father's amazing collection of African art books and began researching. Often these glossy, coffee-table affairs were way too heavy for me to hold, but I persevered. I read voraciously. And the more I wrote, the better I felt. On good days, the feeling of gloom gave way to a driving streak of ambition and accomplishment. I scraped together whatever strength I had, sat at my computer and wrote. With each page, I thought of new ideas. It was as though an unknown journey was unfolding before me. With each door I creaked open, a few more opened ahead of me. I was travelling the continent from the prison of my teenage bedroom. I was voyaging inside my head and it was miraculous.

SPACE

27 January 2004

A YEAR BEFORE I GOT sick, I spent two years living in New York City. It was a terrifying time but an exhilarating one. I lived from day to day, struggling to make it as a journalist and earning my keep as a waiter and a stylist at the same time. In between, I explored the immense cultural variety and sexual liberties of the city. Walking down Fifth Avenue among the skyscrapers, I felt part of the greatest city on earth. From way out on the periphery, I had honed in on the centre of the universe. Everything around me seemed to have some global significance.

As time passed I grew exhausted with the struggle to break into the New York scene. After eighteen months I had earned precisely $550 from journalism and had made two friends. I was no more part of the system than a Pakistani cab driver or a Mexican dishwasher. Slowly it began to dawn on me that there was a price to pay for this privilege. Sure, I could leapfrog my way to the centre of the world, but without immigration papers it would take forever for me to establish any identity or reputation for myself within that centre. Here I was in the most significant place on the planet, and yet never had I felt more insignificant.

On my rare days off, I'd walk the city streets or cycle in Central Park, but more and more I became aware of my deep sense of alienation. I thought about coming home. The idea carried with it a great sense of failure. Like so many others, I had come to New York with a dream, and like so many others', my dream had not become a reality. I felt deeply torn. Frustrated as I was growing with my lack of progress, I knew how much I would be giving up by leaving. The visits to museums, the talks by famous authors, the fabulous dance parties, the thrill of utter independence – simply being able to hop on a subway and go anywhere. How on earth would parochial little Johannesburg begin to compete? I spoke with my wise friend, Emerson, a New Yorker who had left the city and was now visiting. 'New York plays tricks on you,' he said. 'It makes you think you can't live without it. But you can.'

I spent my last two weeks in New York, obsessed with completing a short film about my friend Kenny. Kenny had come to New York with dreams of becoming a dancer, but twelve years later he was still a waiter, and now an alcoholic. We stayed up many nights interviewing the ageing barflies and homeless people, who all had similar stories to his. I called the film *Losers*, in tribute to all the losers whose only success in life had been to migrate to this seductive metropolis. Kenny spoke into the camera, in silhouette against the deserted 3 a.m. streets of the West Village. 'The real loser here is the filmmaker,' he said. 'Because he thinks, just because he hasn't made it here yet, he's failed.' He was right in a sense, but I knew that by admitting to that failure, I was giving myself an opportunity to win somewhere else. Only how would I ever know that I'd won?

For a good few years before my Manhattan experiment, I had gobbled up the African continent. I had embarked on wondrous adventures that few ever had the chance to experience – crossing the desert by camel, seeking out demented old chiefs, artists and visionaries, hunkering down in the bush with East Africa's last hunter-gatherers. My experiences had been so much broader and more unlikely than my contemporaries'. For months, I would simply trace out my passions on the map and follow them, unhindered by geography, social norms or hardships. Never had I felt so free. I made long arduous journeys, and eventually I would slouch out on a hammock in a tiny town in the middle of nowhere – a place no one had ever heard of, places of no significance whatsoever – and smile with satisfaction. And in these tiny places I'd begun to feel bigger. I had covered such great distances and traversed such immense cultural divides that I felt like a giant.

In time, this too had begun to exhaust me. Visiting places for a second or third time, I grew aware of how horribly paralysed they were, and how little chance the people I'd met had of making any changes to their lives. This had begun to distress me. The romance of exotic travel began to wear off and, more and more, I spent time in my house in Johannesburg.

Every time I returned to the city of my birth, I would descend into a maudlin state. No sooner had the thrill of seeing my loved ones worn off, I'd find myself driving home miserable on Saturday nights, thinking about how few options there were for entertainment and how small-minded the people I often encountered were. More and more, I felt part of an insignificant minority, unable to connect with mainstream culture and unable to find any subculture in which I felt at home. Sometimes I'd miss the Sahara – how much wilder and bolder had such adventures been? This all seemed so dreadfully suburban and mediocre.

At other times, I missed New York just as deeply. Johannesburg was simply not Manhattan. From a thousand options per night, I was down to one or two. From a universe of souls, I was down to the same miserable faces I had seen since primary school. This, too, seemed to me the apex of mediocrity.

Getting ill took me totally by surprise. The physical pain, the extreme lifestyle changes, the pressure it placed on all my relationships and the tremendous sense of dependency it entailed all conspired to a state of utter confusion. It had taken a good four months for me to fathom what was happening to me. Only now had I begun to contemplate the consequences.

The days had grown longer. The visits from friends had grown fewer. Often I would see no one but my parents and the occasional doctor for a week or two. And, lying alone on my bed on those interminable afternoons, I would contemplate the four walls around me.

I had personalised the space over the past months. There was a bulbous African mask, a kitsch Chinese Mao plaque and a pink plastic take on an African stool that brought me much delight. The antique entomological prints had made way for a couple of naive landscape paintings I'd bought on the side of the road. There was also a bookshelf, piled proudly with my research and review books. The room was a little tackier, but much more me.

But still, the space had become something of a prison. On many days I was too weak to leave the room, let alone the house. Some days I kept the curtains drawn and had no idea whether or not the sun had shone. From the endless vistas of sand dunes to the impossible towering of skyscrapers, and now to this – a tiny, intransient universe, hopelessly cut off from everywhere and everyone.

And then something very strange struck me. Here, in this tiny prison, a heart still thumped inside my chest. Had you asked me a year earlier how I would cope with being cooped up like a solitary chicken for months, I'd have told you it sounded worse than death. Without the freedom to go anywhere one chose or do what one wanted, what was there in life? And yet now I had surprised myself. I had learnt that we can never imagine how we will respond to a situation until we're faced with it. That our powers of adaptation are far more powerful than we imagine. That there are so many things that make us think we can't live without them.

But we can.

POISONED

28 January 2004

MOM CAME HOME EARLY from work. She said Elsie's daughter, Sophie, had been to see her. We had tried to contact Elsie a few times, but without success. Sophie said that Elsie had coughed more and more, but they had got her some herbs from the sangoma, which helped a little. But she just kept getting thinner and she couldn't get out of bed. Her mother had been poisoned, Sophie said, so there wasn't any point in going to the clinic. They just used the herbs, but these had stopped working, and she'd started coughing up blood. Sometime in November, they'd lost her. It was a blessing, Sophie said. She had been suffering. And what can you do if someone has poisoned you?

I remembered our little trip to the bus stop, Elsie and I, twinned in our denial. Yes, I'd finally had the courage to challenge mine, but I'd also had a whole lot of information and support that allowed me to do so. Elsie had none of that. And, even if she *had* felt a sufficient sense of urgency to finally resort to Western medicine, what were her chances of survival? Aids never strikes in isolation. It strikes in a context of economics and infrastructure and belief systems. And most often it is that context rather than the disease itself that determines one's chance of survival. It was Elsie's misfortune to have been born into a context of poverty and ignorance. And that had killed her. And *that*, as I was beginning to grasp, was the poison.

CELEB

29 January 2004

A FEW DAYS LATER, I received a call from my friend Carl. He was preparing a photographic exhibition of people living with Aids and he wanted to photograph me. I was unsure about this. Initially, I had defended my right to privacy quite fiercely. At one point I had suggested writing a piece about my illness for the newspaper, but then changed my mind. I simply wasn't ready for that level of public glare. Apart from all the gossip that would ensue, such an act might launch me publicly as an activist – a task I was unsure I had the strength for at that stage.

I was also beginning a career as an author and was worried about being typecast as 'that Aids victim with a story to tell'. I would far rather be the author who happened to have Aids. One day, perhaps, I might publish a book about all this, I figured – a simple memoir, detailing the daily trials of the disease that so few people seemed at all familiar with. One day, perhaps, but not right then.

Gradually, however, it had dawned on me that pretty much everyone in my life knew what was going on by then. I had also worked through any subconscious feelings of shame. Not only was there no shame in suffering this disease, there was pride in fighting it. I quizzed Carl carefully on how broad the exposure would be. Satisfied, I agreed to meet the following day.

Lately I'd been battling more and more with my self-image. A few wisps of hair had already begun falling out, my skin was sallow and there was still hardly any flesh on me. This was not to be a glamour shot, but, hey, it might just be a meaningful experience. I posed in my parents' living room, in front of their African art collection. Carl wanted to show that the disease affected middle-class people as well as the poor. 'So what are you looking for?' I asked. 'A Sarajevo expression?'

'No, I don't want you looking like a victim. Hold your head up.'

I did so for a few shots, and then I did something very brave. Spontaneously, I took off my shirt. I knew this was completely unflattering, frightening even. My skeletal ribs, my tiny waist, my pale skin … and yet I felt that if the portrait could embody both dignity and honesty, my nakedness would make it all the more powerful. I also hoped that by coming out, I might help others to do the same and might help chip away at the conspiracy of silence. I was pleased I had done this.

Later, I got to see a photo of some skeleton, laughing cheerily. It was me, and it worked. I felt liberated. 'D'you know what?' I said to Carl. 'I think I *am* going to publish the memoir I've been scribbling, after all. I don't care who knows any more. I think there's room for some kind of journal. Simply written. Just detailing what can happen and how it makes you feel. I'll speak to my publishers about it. Who knows? Maybe it could be useful.'

BLOOD

10 February 2004

WITH EACH PASSING DAY, I felt weaker. I'd write for a half an hour or so in the mornings and then collapse into bed. I knew I was spending far too much time lying on my back, but there was little I could do about it. I dressed warmly and Mom bundled me into the car and took me for blood tests. The following day, Dr D called Mom about the results. I was chatting with Alex when she broke the news to me. I'd been hoping to go out for lunch the following day. 'I'm afraid we won't be going for lunch tomorrow,' Mom announced. 'You need to have a blood transfusion.'

I grimaced. D had suggested this once before, and I'd made a big fuss. For some reason, it seemed even scarier and more invasive than the chemotherapy. Whose alien bodily fluids was I to welcome into my veins? 'Oh God, do I have to?' I protested.

'Yes, I'm afraid you do,' she said softly. 'And D says you'll feel much better afterwards.'

It seemed so unfair – it was either the chemo or the combination of ARVs and antibiotics that was playing havoc with my blood levels. A red blood cell count – or haemoglobin levels – should be between 14 and 18 in an adult male. Mine had dropped to 6.1. No wonder I felt wasted. I could hardly argue against the transfusion. Nevertheless, I maintained a grumpy mood in protest for the rest of the day. It was agreed that I would have the transfusion overnight in hospital – that way I could sleep while the precious life liquid dripped into my veins. I needed three pints of blood, which would take around nine hours to administer.

The following day, my parents took me to the hospital. Again, the stench of germs and medicine assaulted me on arrival. I waited a couple of hours while a nurse went to source my blood. She returned with a cold, dark red bag that had come out of some anonymous body. I was shivering. 'Okay, let's do it,' she said.

I resisted. I knew that a thicker needle was required and that it was likely to hurt. She pushed the spike into my arm, and my screams echoed down the corridor. There was no way I could take nine hours of this. 'Get it out of me!' I yelled.

As it turned out, she was inexperienced and had inserted the needle into tissue instead of a vein. My whole body was shaking violently. I demanded someone more superior. The sister arrived promptly. Could she wait till I stopped shaking? I pleaded. 'Well, okay, a few minutes. But we need to get moving – your blood levels are very low.'

The sister inserted the needle. It was agony, but nothing like the previous attempt. The other nurse sulked in the background. I glared at her. And then, very slowly, the first bag of salvatory haemoglobin began to drip, drip, drip.

What followed was one of the worst ordeals I have ever been subjected to. The blood passed very slowly into my arm. Around 11 p.m., we were onto the second bag. I couldn't sleep. I just lay there, in the dim light, watching each drop of this alien substance drip into me. After half an hour, I switched on the light. The blood had stopped. I rang for the night nurse. She fiddled a little, but to no avail. She would have to reinsert the needle. I cringed. She jabbed me twice before finding a suitable vein, and presently the tedious flow commenced.

Around 2 a.m., it happened again. I was furious. They hadn't been checking up on me. Had I actually fallen asleep, I would have simply lain there, spiked up to an empty tube. She fiddled and the blood began to flow, but very slowly. It was 3 a.m. before we plugged in the final bag.

By 6.30, I could take it no longer. I was insistent. 'You've got to get this out of me.' There was a little blood left, but the exhausted night nurse relented. It had now been fifteen hours and I couldn't take another moment of it.

Mom and Dad arrived at seven. Soon afterwards, I broke into a bed-drenching sweat. I dried myself and waited an hour as prescribed, and my parents drove me home. It had been pure hell. I collapsed and slept all day.

Little did I realise, there was another nasty little surprise awaiting me. The transfusion had resulted in swelling, and gravity being what it is, the swelling had plummeted directly to my already aching feet. The antidote was exercise – not exactly my forte in my present state of immobility. That, and waiting. And aching. It would be a good few days before I felt any brighter.

FRIENDS

15 February 2004

DAD AND I WEREN'T all that close while I was growing up. Admittedly, I had been quite a handful during my teenage years. I was arty and fiercely rebellious. I swanned around pretentiously in berets, puffing on long brown Dumont cigarettes and listening to Rickie Lee Jones. Toss in my deviant sexuality and growing marijuana habit and, on a 1-10 adolescent difficulty scale, I was probably a decent eight and a half.

Dad was difficult too. His career was placing huge demands on him at the time, so he worked very hard. The little free time he had to spend with his family, he was often withdrawn and glued to his drawing board or the TV set.

Mom added fuel to the fire. With the very best intentions, she always stood between us. If I misbehaved, she'd help me conceal the evidence – partly to protect me from Dad's wrath and partly to save him the annoyance. As a result, however, we had very few confrontations. Issues were brushed neatly under the kilims in the living room and the placid mood belied a permanently tense subtext.

Mom and I had always enjoyed a far easier relationship. She had always been a dedicated mother, schlepping my sisters and me around, attending to our fussy needs and wearing herself down to the bone. While we skirted around any deep or prickly issues, on the surface we had always got along well.

When I returned to Johannesburg from three years at university in Cape Town, the situation began to improve. I had matured somewhat. I had also come out to my parents and had far less to hide. As the tension eased, Dad and I began discovering some common ground. We were both interested in world music, books, African art and design, and, as we began to discover, we had plenty to talk about.

I was not living at home and was happy to be independent. Sometimes, Dad would get upset if I hadn't called or visited for a while, but every fortnight or so, I'd make sure I was home for Friday night dinner – a tradition that had far more to do with burnt chicken than with religion. Intellectually, the conversation was fluid and interesting, but, beyond that, there was little emotional expression.

I knew all this because I was in the midst of years of regressive psychotherapy, complete with all the attendant critiques of one's upbringing. The accusations my therapist launched at Mom and Dad alarmed me at first, but gradually they helped me to separate what had been detrimental to my growth and what had been true expressions of love and generosity.

During my two-year sojourn in New York, the physical

distance had placed a strain on our relationships, but our e-mails became more intimate, and when I finally returned, we simply picked up where we'd left off. They were relieved I was home and we were all more relaxed with one another, but they were still very much my parents. The traditional roles were rarely broken. I'd visit them, but we wouldn't go to movies together and I never hung out with them and my friends at the same time. There were friends and there were parents. And there were sisters living too far away in Cape Town.

I got along with both of them, but over the past few years I'd grown very close to my younger sister, Alli. She shared my rebellious streak and my rejection of mainstream culture and materialism. She'd worn dreadlocks for a while, but now limited her Boho leanings to the odd Indian top. We shared music and fashion tastes. She liked travelling and she liked getting stoned, and, of course, so did I. Over the years, she had shifted from 'sister' to 'friend'.

Cathi, my other sister, and I had had little opportunity for intimacy lately. She was deeply concerned about my situation, but unfortunately had developed a deep phobia of flying. She also had her hands full raising her first child. Because I was too ill to travel, we had scarcely seen each other since her wedding eighteen months before. Alli had flown up to see me in November, but I had been so ill, we had hardly talked. I barely remembered her visit. Now, she was scheduled for another one.

As always, I was delighted to see her. She brought a certain calmness with her, and despite my current state of fear and discomfort, it was a tonic, sitting with her and chatting. As often, the subject of Mom and Dad came up for discussion. We agreed how much Dad had softened over the years; how, as his silver crop had paled to white, he had become so much more gentle and approachable. But for me, something more had happened. Besides for the obvious reasons of physical proximity and the terrors of illness that had brought us closer, in the absence of distractions and denial, both Mom and Dad had spent many hours with me, filling me in on the details of their days and listening to my difficulties with my friends or my writing.

Dad's time was around 6 p.m. He'd come and sit in my room and we'd yak away. He was a great help for the African art book, and listened sensitively when I expressed my emotional state. Mom's time was around 7.30, after she'd survived the ordeal of preparing my meals. She'd come and eat with me and we'd post-mortem the day. But Mom's gifts came in actions more than words. Her tireless preparations of meals, sometimes two or three attempts, for the nauseous patient. Her fastidious stocking and preparation of my pills twice a day. Her schlepping to buy me anything I needed or take me anywhere I needed to go.

'Hey, Al,' I told my sister. 'It's amazing. They are the most dedicated parents. Only now, we've also become friends.'

JENNY

2 April 2004

I WENT IN FOR MY second course of chemo. It was easier this time, knowing what I was in for. My greatest fear, I had learnt, was my fear of the unknown. What I knew was manageable somehow. I'd begun to build up a good rapport with the nurses. It was such a comfort to see them. They had that great mixture of kindness and wit, with a little mischief to go. At times, they'd hustle me into the backyard, wheeling my drip in tow, so we could all have a cigarette in their secret spot.

I paid a routine visit to Dr D the following week. As I was leaving, I saw a woman being wheeled in in a chair. I had been toying with the thought of getting a wheelchair lately. Mercifully, I was able to walk, but it was a terrible strain on my feet. With a chair, I could cover longer distances and have more freedom. I approached her. 'Do you know where I can buy a second-hand wheelchair?' I asked. 'Yes, there are various places,' she replied. 'Why don't you call me later? Get my number from Dr D. My name's Jenny.'

I phoned and left a message, and she called me back that evening. She ran me through some of the options, and then asked what was wrong with me. I dragged her through my list of illnesses. 'And what about you?' I asked.

'I've got MS,' she said. 'Multiple sclerosis. I can't do anything for myself. I can't even move my baby finger.'

'Oh, God! You're incredibly brave,' I said.

'Well, what choice do I have?' she replied. 'I've been

this way for fifteen years, eight of them in total paralysis. And the worst thing about it is there's nothing they can do for me.'

'Can't they at least make your life a little more tolerable?'

'Not really,' she said. 'But I can do that, and I do. And d'you know how? … I make sure I'm out there as much as I can be. I go everywhere in this chair.'

'It's just the stigma that worries me, I suppose,' I said, voicing a concern I'd had for a while. 'The stares. The whispering.'

'Oh, they can fuck off,' Jenny blurted out, surprisingly. 'Really, the people who love you will love you regardless; as for the others, I don't give a damn … Get yourself a chair. Get out there. Live! It offers you so many more options. Can you feed yourself?'

'Yes.'

'Well, I can't, but you can. So go. Go out for coffee. Go to Norwood. Meet people. You can hold a cup. Do it.'

I was humbled. My own limitations seemed absolutely trivial in comparison with hers. Just how a human being could sustain such tremendous suffering and frustration for so long, without a shred of hope to cling to, was utterly beyond me. What stamina! How, when one's quality of life had diminished so immensely, could one find the strength to continue? How could one see any justice in the world? How could one avoid drowning in self-pity? Worse still, unable even to execute one's suicide, how could one sustain the years of torture?

The questions were rhetorical. The answers lay not in words, but in the examples of people like Jenny, who had retained her dignity and positivity in the most cruel darkness imaginable. 'You have been an amazing inspiration to me,' I said. 'Thank you.'

'Get that chair,' she said. It was the first and last time I spoke to her. A few months later, I read in the paper that she'd died. 'Yes,' said D. 'Mercifully. That's the worst thing about MS. It just takes far too long. By the end, she could only move her eyelids.'

* * *

I checked out various wheelchair options, when, quite serendipitously, a relative offered to lend me a chair she no longer required. Dad went to fetch it and left a note on my door. 'Your chariot awaits you.'

Come Saturday afternoon, I was ready for my first outing – a wheel around Zoo Lake. I felt pretty weak, but both Alex and Mom had offered to take me out, so I pulled myself together, swallowed an extra morphine tablet and waited as they struggled to get the weighty chunk of metal into the car. It wasn't happening. The back seat. The boot. Another car. Eventually we were ready to depart.

When we arrived, the cushion for the chair had mysteriously disappeared. This meant serious discomfort for my bony ass. I climbed into the chair. While these were all very well for people with no sensation in their legs, I had not bargained for the effect the tiniest bumps in the sidewalk would have on my feet. The further we rolled, the more I grimaced.

Soon enough I encountered my first stares. Spontaneously, I began making moronic noises and shaking my arms about. They want to stare, I'll give 'em something to stare at, I figured defensively. I'll terrify them. Mom and Alex were terribly embarrassed, but they persevered, wheeling the grumbling monster around the lake.

All along, the conversation remained tense. Eventually we pulled up to a restaurant, where the toasted cheese I ordered was quite the most unpalatable lump of slime you could imagine. To top it, a small swarm of bees descended on us and we spent the next fifteen minutes shuffling around the cool drinks and shooing them away. 'Um, I think I'd like to go home now,' I groaned.

By the time we got home, Alex had lost it. My impatience with Mom, my general rudeness and ingratitude had upset her, and she was quite emotional. 'Okay, Addie,' she levelled. 'A disaster! I understand you're in pain, but can't you try and contain your moods?' She was angry and upset. 'Okay then,' she shrugged. 'We'll try again another time.'

I felt awful. Since my father had expressed his hurt, I had endeavoured to treat everyone as kindly as they were treating me. The problem with depending on others lay in how to make the necessary demands without behaving like an utter brat. 'Stop the chair. No, turn it. Ouch! My feet! Slower! Quicker!!' I was surprised they hadn't chucked me into the lake.

* * *

My next round of chemo went smoothly enough. There was nothing pleasant about it, but, somehow, I was getting used to it. The side effects were another matter. My eating schedules were unpredictable. Sometimes I couldn't eat in the mornings, sometimes at night, sometimes not at all. Most foods tasted utterly toxic. Cheese, my favourite, became a monster. Cereal was like gravel. Bread like wood. I could hardly afford to lose another ten grams, and yet on many days I could scarcely manage to force anything down. A little soup perhaps. A kiddies' portion at night. For some weird reason, for a few days after each session, I was cursed with days of incessant hiccoughing that jolted my sensitive frame, like an interminable journey on a goods train. All of this left me feeling even weaker.

Indeed, by that stage, my body felt so frail, I was terrified to look at it. Over the months, I had developed so many fears and I had allowed those fears to get bigger and bigger. Drying myself was scary – as if the slightest brush of a towel might rip off a chunk of my delicate skin. Even water frightened me. Wetness, hot, cold, movement had all become monsters. My fragility had overwhelmed me to the degree that I'd become petrified of my own body … And yes, my bloods had dropped again. I would need another transfusion.

CHARLES

26 April 2004

THE FOLLOWING TRANSFUSION WENT far more smoothly. I chose to have it at the oncology centre, and my magical, highly skilled and faithful nurses got me through the ordeal with little discomfort. This was two pints of blood instead of three, yet instead of fifteen hours, they pulled it off in three and a half.

The side effects were also far less severe, and two days later I was well enough for a coffee with someone I had never met. My parents had suggested this and I had agreed. The man's name was Charles. My parents had known him long ago, but had lost contact. Charles had contracted Aids a decade before and had come very close to death. Ten years later, he was living a full and rewarding life. He was in town on business and had kindly offered to come and see me.

I propped myself up in the living room. Charles greeted me warmly. Wow, he looked pretty damn normal. Slim but not skeletal. Grey hair, glowing skin. Agile. If you didn't know it, you'd never have guessed what he'd been through. There was so much I wanted to ask him. There had been so many questions, such uncertainty and so little information. I began my quiz.

'How bad did it get?'

'Well, very close to death, my friend. I developed meningitis at one point and was in a coma for three months. I had strokes. Loads of infections. It took me forever to recover. Really, it was around three years before I was living with any kind of normality.'

'Did you have neuropathy?' He shook his head. 'I *still* have neuropathy. It's remarkably better, but the nights are still awful sometimes. I can't wear shoes for too long. At one point, you couldn't lay a piece of paper on my feet without me screaming. But, very slowly, it's improved.'

Charles answered a long list of questions. I could have

asked Dr D, but it wouldn't have been the same. Here was someone who had been through it and was still going through it, but he was winning. He still battled with his anti-retrovirals, he said. He ate twice as much as anyone else, he claimed, but remained skinny. And yet, for the most part, he was able to function normally and enjoyed a decent quality of life.

He hugged me warmly. 'If there's one thing I want to leave you with,' he said, 'it's this – *everything* gets better. It takes forever, but it happens. Your CD4 count rises. You get stronger. Less vulnerable. You suffer less. Trust me. You're doing fine. Just hang in there.'

I waved as Charles reversed his car down the driveway. It had been such a relief to finally encounter some genuine empathy. The fact that there were millions of Aids victims and survivors around the world meant very little, because through all of this, I hadn't met anyone who'd truly experienced the depths of my fears or who knew the extent of my pain. For all the love and caring around me, I had felt so very alone. Now I knew I wasn't. Disturbed as I was that Charles still suffered, I was delighted to see him walking normally, wearing shoes and driving a car. What I'd been told so many times finally seemed plausible. Aids was a life sentence, but a manageable one.

I felt a little better the following week, so I called my friend Roy and invited him out for lunch. He was amazed at my sudden burst of energy, and we wolfed down a Thai meal and marched around the malls, snapping up clothing and CDs. I walked far further than I had in the previous couple of months and was exhilarated just to be out and about. As we drove home, Roy seemed a little flat. 'What's up?' I asked.

'Didn't you see?'

'See what?

'Those people. The way they were fucking staring at you. It made me so angry.'

No, I hadn't seen. I'd grown so used to the vision of my pale, emaciated self, shuffling along, it had become quite normal to me. I'd also been so excited to be out and about, I'd just forged on past the pitiful stares, unaware of anything. But Roy's observation offered me some very useful insight.

Just as I was familiar with my obviously strange appearance, so too were those people I used to find it impossible to avoid staring at. That retarded child, that armless woman – not only had they all seen themselves in the mirror for years, they'd also been subject to the same awkward stares wherever they went. What was so compellingly unfamiliar to us was all totally predictable to them. And now it was becoming familiar to me. I offered Roy the extraordinary slice of wisdom that extraordinary quadriplegic spirit had taught me from her wheelchair, 'Oh, them? They can just fuck off!'

HEELS
7 May 2004

Few souls could keep up with the ridiculous social antics of my drag gang, but the odd lunatic left us totally in the shade. One such hero was a hairdresser who went by the name of Henry Heels. Heels was something of a performance artist. Although his acts were generally too far gone to draw much popular support, among a few of us, Heels was a legend. On one occasion, dressed in standard six-inch platforms, Heels arrived at the club with packets of pigs' intestine he intended to lather about himself to a Marilyn Manson track. It was Heels' twisted idea of drag, but the generally liberal management drew the line and Heels stormed out in a huff with the intestines in tow. 'But you promised us ...' he snorted loudly at the owner as he left. 'You promised us a *progressive* club!'

It was of no great surprise, but of great sadness when we learnt a few months later that Heels had popped too many Ecstasy tabs one night, and had passed out and choked on his own vomit. The funeral service was dreadful. It took place in a conservative church among a batch of stiff family members who wouldn't acknowledge the fact that he was gay. The only inkling of Heels' presence came after the sermon, when the family insisted on playing some dreadful hymns. For some reason, the CD kept sticking. This was Heels' work and we knew it. The more the CD jumped, the more we all chuckled under our breath, and eventually the whole incongruous clutch of clubbers in the two back rows just burst into applause.

As far as I was concerned, this was not a satisfactory tribute to a legend, and so, the following day, I made my way down to the second-hand store and bought as many nasty pairs of used high heels I could lay my eyes on. I took them home, smoked a joint and got out my paintbrushes. Each shoe was given a word that reminded me of Heels. Gorgeous. Lipstick. Bitch. Happy. Insane. Bitch. Lame. Screaming. Relentless. A hundred shoes later, I called Jan and Albert with the plot.

Saturday evening, they arrived at my house with a tree in the back of their Land Rover. We made our way to the club around midnight. The folks at the door had come to expect almost anything, but the last thing they expected was to see us storming in with a tree in tow. Generally, however, if you look like you know what you're doing and you have a reputation for entertainment, no one stops you, and so, soon enough, we had assembled the tree in the lobby and adorned it with the heels of tribute.

As the night progressed, friends plucked heels off the tree. They held their drinks in them, tossed them around the dance floor and limped about screaming in delight. Many people walked off with a heel or two as a memento. Dizzy. Unforgettable. Hairspray. Baby. Bitch. We partied frantically until sunrise, at which point I passed out in the back of the Land Rover. As we pulled off, I looked up at the pink dawn sky into the canopy of Jacaranda trees outside the club's entrance. And through my inebriated daze, I could see that their branches were strewn triumphantly with shoes.

BONE
9 May 2004

THE NEWS OF HEELS' death was broken to me on a Sunday evening at a crummy little bar called Moon Café. Heels had come home around seven that morning and passed out in Clinton the DJ's bed. A couple of hours later, Clinton woke up and realised that Heels wasn't breathing. I literally collapsed on the floor when I heard the news. As huge as the risks were that he'd insisted on taking, he had always been so full of vitality, it seemed impossible that he was gone.

I went to the bar and ordered a beer. Moon, for all its crumminess, was my favourite venue at that stage. It was owned and run, seven days a week, by two of my favourite people at that time – the legendary queen of trashy drag royalty, Miss Sharon Bone, and her bearded, bandanna-wearing boyfriend, Andrew. We often wondered what was under that bandanna, but to this day we've never found out.

Bone was not your standard female impersonator. Tall, skinny and with a pronounced limp, she wasn't an ideal entertainer either. Blessed as she was with extremely large eyes, a strong jaw and a prominent missing tooth, nor was she your standard beauty, but Miss Bone had her own plan, and from the start she was destined for underground stardom. For those who encountered her for the first time, scowling her substandard lip-synch and flapping those long skinny arms in a bad glitter boob-tube, gauzy mini and patchwork leather court shoes to the Andrews Sisters, she must have been quite frightening, but to those who had come to love and admire her, Bone was pure genius. She was also something of a darling.

Andrew was a nightly fixture behind the bar. He simply poured the drinks and chatted, while Bone played the role of hostess. Most nights around ten, she and her little crew would mount the makeshift stage in the corner of the bar and perform a few numbers.

Often I'd sneak backstage beforehand and hang out with the crew. While the others had clear aspirations of upping the glamour stakes and crossing the gender divide, Bone was evidently motivated by different concerns. Her act was usually a shocker. Her wardrobe was a large heap of ill-fitting second-hand frocks. There were moments of disco extravaganza, frumpy hausfrau, uptight nurse, and many other unimaginable incarnations.

Just before show time, she'd fish something out of the heap and pull it on in some ghastly way. She might tie on a spangled scarf somewhere as token glamour.

Next up – hair. Bone's wigs were generally in a tatty state of repair. As the night wore on, she'd turn them inside out or back to front or simply rip them off and fling them at the crowd. The make-up was another story. Depending on how out of it she was when she applied it, it ran the gamut from gaudy to utterly grotesque. The already bulging eyes got bigger. On a good night, the lips too were enlarged with a liner and then plastered with red glitter. On a bad night, there were disturbing lines or strange shapes painted onto the cheeks and forehead. Her look complete, Bone would grab a CD and then hurry on stage. There were times she forgot the words, or the CD got stuck, but it never mattered. Bone had everything required to pull it off.

The layout at Moon was most unusual. An abandoned shopfront at the intersection of two busy roads comprised a downstairs performance space. Four floors up, in the deserted building, a three-bedroom flat had been converted into a second bar. The crowd was anything but glamorous. Creepy, dishevelled old men sat downing their brandies and Cokes, while the odd trendies hung about for the irony. Regardless, there was something truly homey about the place, and when they were finally forced to move, the regulars were distraught.

The New Moon, as it was called, was bigger and better situated, bang in the heart of the popular gay strip. The crowd simply moved over as if nothing had happened. Bone scowled and jerked her spidery arms about. One attractive look she came up with involved a frumpy brown mini, a pair of laddered stockings and no underwear. Whenever Bone got to the chorus, she'd raise her hands above her head, revealing her stockinged privates to shrieks of horror. Her blank expressions were quite priceless.

Bone stopped at nothing. One night, on the dance floor at Therapy, the slick, relentless thumper of a dance club across the road, Bone stripped stark naked in the middle of a song. Bone was not *Playgirl* material, and for the more uptight among us, the move was truly offensive. As a result, Miss Sharon Bone was banned from the establishment, but this simply won her more kudos with the hard-core rebels.

On rare occasions, I rose to the challenge of joining Miss Bone's ensemble cast of deluded divas and fierce transvestite punks. Every now and then, I'd arrive in an afro, a tight-fitting cocktail dress, with my exposed extremities lathered in cheap black shoe polish. 'We have a special guest appearing tonight,' Bone would announce in her habitual deadpan drawl. 'Mrs Schwartz!' I would proceed to kneel, tumble and prostrate myself while lip-synching amateurishly to some soaring gospel number, collapsing on cue to the final hallelujahs. And for the select few who found it amusing, it was worth the trouble.

On the weekend before I left for New York, we partied like Trojans. By Sunday morning, Bone and Andrew had closed up their club and Bone and I sat on the kitchen floor in the dawn light, sniffing slivers of cocaine. It was a blurry but intimate moment. All my life, I had held the greatest respect for those brave individuals who didn't give a tin of paint what people said, but celebrated life and their own freakishness with gusto. Bone was one such warrior. Brave, original and demented. And later, long after I had lost touch with this barbaric crew, as I lay curled up in the foetal position on my bed, praying for my recovery, it was to precious memories like these that I turned for my solace.

* * *

I missed this life. I missed being part of a gang and being mischievous. Socially inept as it was, it was actually one of my better behavioural patterns, for within this crew, everything was up front. Our lives were all so closely woven together, there was little space to be sneaking around. It was a naughty existence, but I felt whole.

I sure enjoyed the notoriety I was earning around Johannesburg, for dishevelled and disgusting as we were, we were certainly the hard-core sideshow on the party circuit.

Now I had simply disappeared. In truth, the gang had begun falling apart before I got ill. Bone and Andrew had mismanaged the New Moon and were now shacked up in a grimy flat in Troyeville. Bone had been forgiven and now worked the Divine Bar at Therapy on the weekends, but the glory days were clearly over.

Jan and Albert's relationship had reduced to a series of petty fights by this stage. It was difficult spending time with the two of them. If one was talking, the other was sulking silently. It reminded me of all the worst things about relationships and I was delighted I wasn't involved with anyone.

Soon after I got ill, I began to lose contact with the crew. Albert, my closest and oldest friend in the gang, remained loyal and paid me weekly visits, during which he'd update me on what I wasn't really missing out on, but the others pretty much disappeared. To be fair, some of the problems were logistical. Bone and Andrew had no car and scarcely ever had any airtime for their phones, let alone cash. They lived on the third floor without an elevator, which was beyond the reach of my feet.

But logistics aside, I also sensed that there was some reluctance on their part to remain interested. Essentially, they were good-time party people, living from day to day, and not worrying about tomorrow. They were also pretty much nocturnal. I, with my disabilities and nightly curfew, wasn't much of a contender for their lifestyle. Much as I had hoped our friendship would hold strong regardless, it hadn't.

My life was so different from theirs. While they were all getting ready to go and cause havoc at the club, I was snuggling down in my bed and watching *Law & Order* with Mom and Dad. I didn't really mind the change in lifestyle. It bored me terribly at times, but mostly I was fine.

One evening, I felt desperate for some reason. It was around 11 p.m. and Mom and Dad were tucked away and the passage light was off. Suddenly I felt so very lost and alone. I missed my wildness, the spontaneity, the excitement. I'd been missing it all for a long time, I guess, but tonight I was able to admit it. I rolled a joint in the bedside light and puffed myself into reverie.

Suddenly I felt wild. I pictured myself doing something crazy, slipping into a blonde wig and onto the wheelchair, and wheeling myself out of the driveway and down the street – embarking on some insane midnight, midweek adventure, as if to affirm some last shred of insane existential freedom.

I scribbled down these thoughts in my notebook, and eventually the burning impulse cooled and I was able to lie down alone in bed and relax. I sedated myself with some gentle music and drifted calmly to sleep.

DAZED

1 June 2004

THE SIDE EFFECTS OF chemotherapy are cumulative. After almost nine months, I was nearing the end of my treatment. Some days I had so little energy I could only manage fifteen minutes at the computer. Each chemo session seemed harder and harder to tolerate. The first couple of hours were okay, but by noon I'd be totally washed out. I'd break into a sweat with the drip in my arm, and get horribly grouchy. I tried to play Scrabble with Mom, but I'd lose patience with it quite quickly. At one point, we kept losing the letters. They'd fallen somewhere between the tubes and the drip stand and my propped-up feet. 'Fuck!' I swore at the top of my voice, oblivious to a room full of fragile cancer patients receiving their medication. 'This fucking Scrabble!'

There remained one session after that one, and the Kaposi's seemed to be under control. In my exhausted state, I had become even more of a burden to the people around me, so the very least I could do was keep up some pretence of coping and do my best to own the word 'positive', or 'POZ', as I preferred. It was only very rarely that I allowed myself to wallow in a state of gloom. But this was one such afternoon.

What had just seemed bearable the previous day now seemed totally beyond me. I was losing patience. My recovery was taking so terribly long, and gradually it was becoming evident that the treatments came with no guarantees. Could I cope with a life full of such pain and uncertainty, I wondered. What quality could it offer me? And was it fucking worth it? When would it get better? When would I get better? Would I ever get better?

Although I'd never thought about it before, I was becoming some kind of survivor, I guess. And yet, there seemed nothing noble or extraordinary about that. It didn't render me some kind of fearless saint, storming through the flames of the Apocalypse. Let's face it – any half-decent idiot with a shred of common sense would have done their best to pull through.

This was the bottom line: They tell you the worst. The very worst. And you find yourself face to face with your greatest fears – not only are you HIV-positive; you have – capital letters – AIDS. A couple of months later, you find out you've got fucking cancer. A month after that, they toss in tuberculosis – *correction*, three different kinds of tuberculosis. You've lost a third of your body weight and your damaged nerves keep you in excruciating pain 24/7. You can hardly stand, let alone walk. Your cancerous eye is bloodshot, and your lesions sting … on your arm, your dick. And you get other pains in weird places. Your hair starts falling out like autumn leaves and you look like some hobbling corpse. So what you gonna do?

You're gonna roll over and say this is just too damn much for me, or you're going to cooperate. You're going to put yourself in the hands of some gifted medical scientists; swallow the buckets of medication they throw at you; humble yourself to the astonishing love, generosity and dedication people are showing you; and do your darnedest to be patient and optimistic and refuse flatly to collapse in some filthy, miserable heap of self-pity.

* * *

All along, people kept asking if all this had changed me. How could it *not* have changed me? It wasn't like I'd found Jesus or something, but, sure, I'd changed. In your average year, there'd be the odd day from hell when you'd figure, 'Hmmn, what would be the least painful? An overdose? Poison? A gun?' But when you see your life dangling on a thread before you, you have no choice but to face the horrifying truth that the entire universe might be snatched violently from you far, far sooner than you'd ever imagined. And so it's simply instinctive that you just grab that thread and clutch on to it with every damn cell in your withering excuse for a body. And *if*, by some ludicrous miracle, you don't kick it, there's no way in hell you're not going to appreciate every breathing second a thousand times more than you ever did before. There's no way you're going to take the same insane risks that you used to. Or be a bitch or a fool. Like I said, there's nothing extraordinary about it. Who wouldn't?

In that process, I guess, I had learnt to change some of the lifestyle patterns that were leading me to a quick spiritual and emotional death. I was no longer ruled by my hungers or desires. My demons had retreated to a safe distance. God, I'll probably kick the bucket for saying this, but fuck it, in some twisted way, it was as though Aids had saved my life.

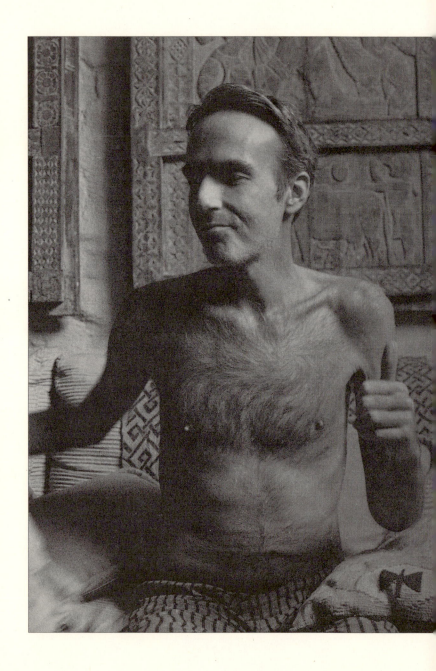

PART TWO
10 December 2004 to 9 January 2005

QUESTIONS

About six months ago, I stopped working on this book. I buried it in the hard drive of my laptop and didn't dare myself the slightest glance at it. But, for fear that my generous daily morphine dose might erase the months completely, I did make a single longhand entry: a series of questions that were plaguing me. I had no answers at that time. But I had an endless quagmire of fears and uncertainties running circles in my mind, and I felt it important to scribble some of them down. The list could have gone on forever, but I allowed myself thirty-five questions — for the thirty-five years I'd managed to battle it out on this planet, and they ran as follows, in random, confusing order:

1. How much will I ever recover? 2. How many of my dreams will I ultimately make happen? 3. Will I always be disabled? 4. If I am, how will I manage my disability? 5. What will I do if Mom and Dad aren't here to help me one day? 6. What will I do if the newspaper folds? 7. How will I make a living if I'm sick? 8. How will I afford my chronic medical needs without my parents' support? 9. What are the chances of me pulling off any immortal achievements from my bedroom? 10. How much of a life can I hope for without full mobility and independence? 11. Will I need to take morphine forever? 12. Will I ever get a hard-on again? 13. Will I ever want one? 14. Will I ever have sex again? 15. With my sore feet, will I ever be able to share a bed with anyone? 16. Will I ever fall in love again? 17. Will I ever experience a

moment without physical pain? 18. Will anyone ever want someone as sick as me? 19. Will I be able to wear a short-sleeved shirt again? 20. Will I ever weigh 75 kilos again? 21. How will I die, peaceful and fulfilled, or miserable and empty? 22. Will I be alone? 23. Will I see New York again? 24. Will I live long enough to write all the books I want to? 25. Will I ever have an African art gallery? 26. Will I make new friends? 27. Will I ever have a six-pack? 28. Will I ever stop smoking? 29. Will I die of emphysema? 30. Where would I be now if none of this had happened? 31. Would I still be searching for intimacy with strangers? 32. Will I ever see the church of Lalibela in Ethiopia? 33. Will I be famous? 34. Will I die before my parents do? 35. After everything I've battled, will I die in a car crash?

On the opposite page I composed a hopeful little mantra.

H.I.V. / Pozitivity / Makes you a fighter / Sets you free.

AVOIDANCE

OTHER THAN THAT, I didn't write a word of this text. There were various reasons for my avoidance. Primarily, I had lost faith in this memoir and had begun to doubt its significance. Who cares? I said to myself. I'm just another one of so many million people in the world with Aids – and most of them are far worse-off than I am. What makes this story worth reading?

I wrestled endlessly with this problem, but ultimately I resolved to complete the book when I was able to, regardless of what universal profundities it might uncover or what literary satisfaction it might give me; I'd write it on the off-chance that someone else might benefit from the information it contained – information that would have helped me immeasurably in clambering through the darkness of this disease. If there was some tiny way in which I could offer something in return for the blessing of my survival, it would be my privilege to do so.

Over a lunch with my publisher, we had discussed another problem. Where does the book end? 'At the end of chemo perhaps?' she suggested. It seemed a feasible place to leave a punctuation mark on a chronic, perhaps terminal disease, but privately I wasn't convinced. I knew that wasn't going to mark any real closure. The story ends at the end of my life, I figured – be that a few months from now, or in forty years. It ends when someone else scrapes together a posthumous memoir out of the mess of notes I've left behind, or when the last page of any book I've ever written gets burnt. That's the end.

Or did the end even matter?

Privately, however, there was a more practical reason for my avoidance. For the first time in this seemingly endless nightmare of stagnation, I appeared to be making some progress. Tentatively, I had begun to usher some normality into the weird trance that had become my life, and I was focusing on the future. For many dark months, working on this memoir had been cathartic for me. Simply writing about this bewildering process as it occurred helped me make sense of it. But, right then, to spend the few vertical hours I was blessed with each day delving back into the utter darkness of my critical days seemed an unhealthy choice. More than anything else at that time, I needed to heal. I needed to learn to live in spite of this disease, rather than trapped inside it. And so, for six months, I didn't type a sentence. Later, I said. When I'm better. Little did I realise how complicated and unpredictable the journey was that lay ahead of me.

As I was soon to discover, the process of managing the disease was not as straightforward as the doctors had led me to believe. Within a few months, everything I'd written about survival being no big deal and just some common, basic, human instinct would seem remarkably glib and naive. If I wanted to stay alive – and there were times when I wasn't all that sure that I did – I was going to have to transcend previously unimaginable suffering and learn to live with an uncertain degree of disability. No matter how things were ultimately going to turn out, I was in for one hell of a fight.

... FOR NOTHING

IN MID-JUNE, SOON AFTER the last chemotherapy needles were extracted from my arm, I paid a visit to Dr D. I was expecting a standard, simple check-up, but it proved far more challenging. He examined me and seemed satisfied with my progress. The cancer appeared to be in remission and my T-cell count had climbed, in three-month intervals, from to 2 to 6 to 35, and was currently a hopeful 76. My weight had increased from a frightening fifty-one kilos to around sixty. It was still a scary sight, but, at last, I was able to look in the mirror.

We discussed the role diet would play in all of this. Half a cup of yellow vegetables each day. Half a cup dark green. Broccoli. Beetroot. They're all good anti-cancer agents. We talked about eating the right foods, instead of just stuffing myself with whatever sticky treats Mom brought home to try to cheer my mood – with my arms still looking like winter twigs, the 'fatten-up-the-Christmas-pig' approach wasn't proving very effective. Nutrition was crucial.

Then D proceeded with some seemingly innocuous questions. 'How often are you bathing?' he asked.

'Well, every now and then,' I replied. 'I mostly just wash with a sponge or a facecloth. It's too difficult getting in and out of the bath.'

'What's wrong with showering?'

'I can't stand in my bare feet on the tiles. It's too painful.'

'Why can't you wear flip-flops?' he countered.

'Yeah, I guess I could try that.'

'I want you to start,' he said sternly. This seemed a strangely intimate area of my life for a professional to be probing, but I had an anxious feeling in the pit of my gut where all this was leading.

'How much are you walking?' he continued.

'Not very much,' I confessed. 'Around the house mostly. Sometimes I go out, but usually it's too sore.'

He took a breath and spoke very calmly. 'Okay. You've been lying in bed for a year now. During all that time, you can build up a lot of fear. You get scared to do things 'cos you can't remember how to do them. Right now, you need to work out how much is literally impossible and how much is really just fear — and the only way you're going to do that is to push yourself beyond your pain threshold. You've got to go beyond the pain … otherwise you'll never know. So, when your feet are sore, you've got to get up and walk on them. I want you to walk ten per cent more this week, and the following week, ten per cent more than that, and so on. Okay? I want you to get out of the house more.'

I paused, wondering how realistic a commitment I could make. 'Okay,' I nodded weakly, 'I'll try it.'

But D wasn't done. 'What about at night? Can you make it to the toilet, or are you using a bucket?'

'No, I have to use a bucket. A jug, actually. My bladder's pretty weak from the pills and my feet are just impossible at night.'

'I want you to stop using it.'

'Really D, I don't know …'

'Well, then you walk to the toilet and empty it after every three times you use it.'

'I don't even know if I can manage that.'

'You *have* to manage that.'

This was a side of D I'd never seen before. He'd never put any pressure on me. He had never been anything but gentle, compassionate and encouraging. Now he was almost shouting. 'Don't you see!? It's *undignified* — lying there, having someone else empty a bucket for you, relying on Mom to take care of everything. I need to start getting you back to some kind of normality. Having a life. Your health is improving, but that's half of it. The other half is you. You have to start challenging all of this. So you get up and you walk on those feet. You fight. You fight to get your life back. 'Cos if you don't, then this has all been for nothing.'

The silence hung heavy in the consultation room. The final phrase had stabbed like a knife. He could have been gentler about it, I figured, as I walked out. Who was this guy? Just some doctor. Okay, *my* doctor. But he had ventured into some very sensitive and personal territory. And his invasion into these intimate corners of the shoddy shred of a life I was clinging onto had embarrassed me greatly. And yet, deep down, I knew he was right.

It was true – what was the point of saving a life, if only to preserve a hopelessly dependent one? What was the point of all the money and pills and suffering if I wasn't going to do my darnedest to reclaim every inch of health and autonomy within my power? I knew there were still so many limits, but I needed to focus less on them and more on the possibilities. I needed to push myself. The pain was there anyway. But I needed to do things in spite of the pain. The point was *doing* them.

And yet, as Mom and I sat down to a post-mortem in a greasy Chinese diner, the journey D had proposed terrified me. What if I failed? What if the medicines worked and I didn't? What if, after all the extraordinary financial and emotional support I'd been blessed with, I didn't have it in me to rise to this overwhelming challenge? And for the first time, as I slurped my way through a less than decent chow mein, I realised that if I had any hope of a decent recovery, it would require my full participation.

THANK YOU

That evening, D's words reeled through my head like a roller-coaster. 'When your feet hurt, then get up and walk on them.' 'Push yourself beyond your pain threshold.' I wondered if he took such liberties with all his patients, and though I never admitted it, secretly I hoped he did, because over the next few days I realised how vital his words had been. I SMSed him a thank-you note. 'You were harsh, D,' I wrote. 'And I thank you for it.'

Slowly, I became aware of some changes. They were tiny – almost invisible to anyone else – but, to me, they were enormous. I was managing to sit up longer in a chair. To work longer. To stave off the inevitable descent into bed until after sunset. To stagger to the kitchen for a midnight bowl of cornflakes. Not only was I coping with some things I hadn't thought possible, the process was changing the way I felt about myself and my future. The prospect of recovery filled me with a forgotten sense of hope.

DRIVING MISS DAISY

Between june and mid-october, I was writing my own little *Guinness Book of Records*. Each week, I was able to do more and more for myself. Though still miserably prostrate at night, with more hours of the day out of bed, I was able to be more productive. I suggested producing a weekly fashion and decor page for the newspaper. My editors were dubious, given my health, but I was determined to prove my usefulness. I was also excited by the project. And so I got busy, conducting interviews, setting up photographs and chasing rogue e-mails from a cordless telephone at my bedside. One day a week, I hobbled in to the office to work on the layout, and I took great pride and enjoyment in fulfilling my new responsibilities. In some weird way, I was beginning to function again.

I hired a housekeeper to prepare my meals and drive me around. Mary was in her fifties and had previously worked for an old lady, taking her for her weekly mauve rinse at the hairdresser and frying fish or schnitzel for her dinner. Kind of Driving Miss Daisy, I guess. At first I felt uncomfortable with this colonial arrangement – it seemed spoilt and indulgent, but I gradually accepted that there were certain tasks I simply wasn't capable of, and I convinced myself that this was simply a requisite step on the journey back to normality, and slowly I began to get used to it all.

I had two choices: pay someone a salary to help me function and reclaim my financial independence; or simply lie back and whither in helplessness. And so Mary drove me to the office, prepared my meals, kept my house in order and helped me up the stairs. And she was good at it. As her résumé attested, she'd had ample experience with old ladies.

As the weeks passed, I learnt to participate in my healing. Armed with a powerful daily dose of morphine, and in spite of the constant pain in my feet, I walked. I sat up and typed, refusing to be confined to my bed. Sitting up was living. Lying down was dying. Vertical life. Horizontal death. And all the while, I was haunted by D's last terrifying phrase: "Cos if you don't, then this has all been for nothing.'

Soon I was able to spend more time at my own house. I pottered about delightedly – hanging pictures, painting objects and heaving around furniture like some ill-advised gym routine. Then, one day, I woke up burning with a somewhat unlikely desire. I asked Mary to drive me to the charity shop, where I dug through a mountain of long-forgotten stilettos, cork wedges and court shoes. After much haggling over price and style, I eventually settled on a lone, weathered navy blue pump, with a bad red and yellow toe detail, which I hustled down to an acceptable R5.

Then, possessed by some throbbing disco urge, I rushed home and chipped a handful of squares off a tatty mirror ball I'd stolen once from a drag queen who owed me money. I glued the squares in place one by one, covering the entire surface of the shoe and finishing off the edges with a strand of fake pearls. I placed my mosaic icon proudly on a side table. A glittering little homage to drag, I thought, but – more than that – a desperate hope that the sheer glamour of an object might help me find something I was looking for. That beauty alone might somehow erase some gloom or relieve some of the pain. And it did.

Day by day, I sifted through the chaos of a house that had been left to other people. I spent many afternoons digging surprises out of trunks and boxes. Objects that told stories of lives I'd forgotten. Photographs, postcards, letters, a little tin doll, a mask, a tiny bottle of sand from the Sahara. I gave them new life, propping them here and there and back here. I clambered on chairs, hammered nails into walls and heaved sofas around with my weak bony frame. I'd move everything, grimace, and then move it all back. I wanted so desperately to create a home again. To place myself in an aesthetic safety zone of mud brown walls and freshly painted peppermint green front doors. And for a few nights I felt safe enough to sleep there, and managed adequately. At thirty-five, I was moving out of home, just as I'd done precisely half a lifetime before.

Through this process, I began to realise that, for all the incredible generosity I had experienced in having people take care of me, to some degree it was hampering my recovery. The more of my power I handed over — by letting Mom prepare my meals, arrange my doctors' appointments and make sense of my baffling daily regimen of pills — the more impotent I felt. I wanted my life back. And the more time I spent in my teenage bedroom, with TV in the evenings and lights out at 10.15 p.m., the harder it would be to reclaim that territory. Very slowly, I was beginning to rediscover my independence.

I was getting better.

FOLDING MESSILY

By the end of October 2004, the newspaper I was working for was in serious trouble. Just as I began to feel that I was able to make a valuable contribution and decently earn my keep, I was faced with the inevitability of a paper in the process of folding. It had been a valiant effort, full of great content and brave, committed people, but it had been dismally mismanaged. Over the past few months, the signs of finality had become impossible to ignore. Gloomy reports had appeared in rival publications. Salaries were being deposited later and later, and freelancers hadn't been paid in months. Creditors were slamming their fists on the doors. One day, the phones were almost cut off; the next, the news services were. And every couple of weeks, the paper shrunk at last-minute notice down to a miserable sixteen pages. It also transpired that, for the past eight months, the company had been diverting our provident fund payments into its own coffers to keep going.

And then, one Monday afternoon, I got a call from Alex with the news we all knew was inevitable. Tomorrow there would be no newspaper.

I remember that last day at the office – ironically, one of the first few that I'd actually managed to be present for a decent number of hours. People were moping about, lost, clutching at books and pot-plants, crying, laughing, doing their utmost to hide from the ravenous reporters who'd come to scoop the drama for the evening news bulletin on TV. The owner addressed us, explaining that this was a short hiatus and that we would meet the following week to decide how we would proceed. But no one believed him.

At around three o'clock, a few of us went to a café nearby for a depressing drink – a yoghurt smoothie and a glum post-mortem that left us all miserable. Having spent most of the year in bed, I couldn't really claim allegiance to the spirit of lost camaraderie around the table. Some people didn't even know who I was. Then, after half an hour, I began feeling some cramps in my stomach and I asked Alex to take me home. She didn't want to be there either.

THE BALLOON

I DIDN'T THINK MUCH OF it – as a morphine addict, I was accustomed to regular bouts of constipation – but the cramps gradually became more acute, and by the following night they had become unbearable. My stomach was so distended, I could feel my abdominal muscles straining to contain it beneath my skin. I felt like a hand grenade waiting to explode. I sat rocking on the edge of my bed, trying to ease the agony, but by 11:30 I was certain I wouldn't make it through the night. Terrified, I called out tentatively to my almost sleeping parents.

'We should have done this hours ago,' Dad grumbled, but they dutifully changed out of their nightclothes, hauled out the car and drove their groaning son to casualty. As the clock ticked into Friday morning, we sat in the yellow light of the waiting room. The glass coffee table offered only sports and health magazines. I asked if there was somewhere I could lie down.

After half an hour, a nerdy young doctor arrived and asked me a few questions.

'What medications are you on?'

I ran him though the interminable list.

'God, why are you on so much morphine?'

'For neuropathy pain! The doctors told me it was totally safe. That I could increase the dose as much as I needed to.'

'Yes, sure. If you're a terminal cancer patient, it's safe. But not if you want to get better. It's killing you.'

With that, he took one look at my ghastly balloon of a stomach and admitted me. I didn't even think about the implications of what he'd just said, 'cos within twenty minutes I was rigged up to a drip, and the flow of antispasmodics into my veins drifted me blissfully into sleep.

DR S

I SPENT FIVE DAYS IN that hospital, with various intravenous substances controlling my discomfort to some degree. I underwent every conceivable X-ray and ultrasound – the technician, it turned out, somehow recognised my gaunt face peeking out of the green hospital frock, from high school. '*I know you!*' she beamed in a nasal twang that took me back to Standard 6. I wasn't in the mood.

The sound showed various distended organs – liver, spleen and especially my lymph nodes, but ultimately the young surgeon could offer me no diagnosis. He discharged me, telling me not to worry and that 'this tummy thing would sort itself out'. My condition had scarcely improved but I went home, hopeful and delighted to escape the ghastly food and the iron regimes of the nursing staff.

But, by the following evening, I was rocking on the edge of my bed again. I made it through the night, and the following morning, D finally arranged for me to see Dr S – a man reputed to be the city's top Aids specialist. Ironically, I had tried to get an appointment with him when I'd first got ill, but had been told there was a three-month waiting list. 'That's just to eliminate the people who want to know if they can get Aids from a toilet seat,' he would tell me later.

An appointment was set for three o'clock. Throughout the day, I felt sicker, and by three I was on the verge of collapse and certain I was unable to bear my poisonous pregnancy a moment longer. I staggered into his office, hunching over my bloated gut, and collapsed onto the plushly upholstered consulting couch. The office was straight out of *Architectural Digest*.

I had lost a good few indispensable kilos in the past weeks and my ribs were poking through my shirt. I was shaking. Suddenly, I felt nauseous and asked for something I could throw up in. The doctor passed me a white porcelain bowl. I sat there, short of breath, terrified, but relieved at the miracle of landing myself in capable hands in what seemed like the nick of time.

Again the questions. 'Why the morphine?'

''Cos the pain was unbearable.'

'But morphine doesn't really work for nerve pain.'

'So why did they give it to me?'

'Out of desperation, I guess. Anything to help you out of your agony.'

'So what's wrong with that? Why's it so dangerous?'

'Because you've become an addict. And gradually you would need more and more of it, and eventually you would have just stopped breathing.'

I digested this information calmly. I knew I had no energy available for anger or regret. We continued.

'Why the chemotherapy?'

'Because I had Kaposi's lesions and I didn't want to die of cancer.'

He looked at the three scars my lesions had left and found two others I hadn't even recognised. 'In fifteen years, I've only sent one patient for chemo, and his lesions were far more advanced than yours were. For chemo, you need to be showing ten new lesions a month. This we could have handled with liquid nitrogen.'

I was speechless. I thought of all those dreadful mornings, dragging myself to the oncology centre, singing to calm myself as the nurses stabbed away at my arm in search of a useable vein. The awful blood transfusions. My body so weakened and poisoned by the chemo, I could barely stagger to the bathroom. Could this really have all been unnecessary? I didn't dare contemplate the rage that would swell up inside me if this were true. I was far too weak to go there. And besides, what if it wasn't? What if Dr S was wrong? What if, without the chemo, I'd be six feet under by now? I dared not look backwards. If I hoped to get through this crisis, I needed to focus all my energy on moving forward.

Within half an hour I was being wheeled into yet another hospital. My fingernails were blue by this stage, and I was white as a sheet of A4. Judging by the ridges on my nails, my weight and my patchy skin, I was severely malnourished, the doctor said. His tentative diagnosis was that one of my atypical TB bacteria had sprung out of control and was gobbling away at my stomach lining. The only way of confirming this was surgery, scheduled for later that afternoon – a laparoscopy, a probe into my awful distended gut to remove some cultures from my lymph nodes and test them for the virus. I remember being wheeled somewhere white and clinical. The green hats of the surgery staff gawking down at me. Some vague explanation from the anaesthetist. Nothing more.

A moment later, I opened my eyes on Mom and Dad.
'When are they going to do it?'
'It's done,' Mom smiled, holding my hand.
'What the hell is in my penis?' I asked the doctor, feeling the sting of a catheter up my urethra. 'Get this damn thing out of me.'
'It's going to sting the next few times you pee,' he told me. And it did. Like razor blades.

GOD BLESS THE WEATHER

THE DAYS THAT FOLLOWED were a nightmare. Not only was I recovering from having the surgeon poke around in my gut, Dr S had decided to wean me off the morphine immediately. I experienced all the excruciating shivers of a hardened, pavement heroin addict going cold turkey. On top of this, without the morphine, the previously just-bearable pain in my feet had reached new extremes. I lay there, with various tubes pumping liquids into me, pleading with the nurses for more painkillers.

The only food I could manage was a big milky bag that dripped insidiously into my arm. As often before, I had diarrhoea. But this time, because of the amount of substances I was receiving, they had attached two heavy monitors to the drip stand. This meant every rush trip to the bathroom was a marathon of unplugging the monitors and hauling twenty kilos of drip down the room with scarcely enough energy to stand. This continued for days.

The physiotherapist arrived and pummelled my chest for phlegm for fear of a pending chest infection. Then we tried some exercises. I lamely stretched out an arm, raised a leg halfway. 'Okay, let's go for a walk,' she said cheerily. She ushered in a walking frame. 'I really don't feel up to it,' I said.

'Come on,' she insisted. 'I have lots of neuropathy patients, and the ones who walk get better, and the ones who don't don't.' I clung determinedly to the frame, but I was so weak and in so much pain that the short journey along the passage seemed interminable. 'Okay,' she chirped, 'let's go around the corner and then come back.' I couldn't.

I remember lying in the hospital bed a few nights later, in my blue paper hospital panties. To ease the pain in my tummy, I'd raise and cross my legs, leaving me staring, in the yellow hospital light, at my bony hope of a shin, coated in areas with a waxy dermatitis – another result of not being able to absorb any nutrients. With my twiggy arms, sunken ribcage and big bloated belly, if I'd had the courage to look in the mirror, my once ample figure probably wouldn't have looked that different from those African kwashiorkor kids they show on the news sometimes, but I didn't.

Dr S's daily visits were seductively reassuring. His suspicions had proved correct, and I was receiving intravenous antibiotics for the TB. He was giving me methadone to wean me off the morphine, as well as a variety of 'safer' painkillers that didn't seem to be working. If it wasn't my tummy, it was my feet, and most of the time it was both. Dr S's soothing words and calming manner never failed to leave me feeling as though everything was going to be all right, until a short while later, when the psychological effects wore off and I'd lie there for the rest of the day twisted into a heap of pain and anxiety.

Alex came to visit. I knew how much she hated hospitals and how frightened she was by the general visceral ambience, but she came anyway. Alex always came. She lent me her stereo and some music she thought I needed. She was right. As I grappled with the horrors of mortality over the next few days, *The Very Best of John Martyn* kept me alive – especially the last song. 'God bless the weather that brought you to me,' he rasped in that timeless, weather-beaten brogue. 'God curse the storm that takes you away.'

It wasn't as though I had any particular special person whom the weather had brought into my life, but the beauty of the poetry moved me immensely. The words stood for every magical soul the wind had ever serendipitously blown towards me, and the dull pain of absence that seemed to inevitably follow. I SMSed the words to a great past love, now living far away in Thailand. And I made it through the dark night. With so much fear and danger hanging in the balance, it felt appropriate to be counting my blessings.

GUESSWORK

I APPEARED TO BE MAKING a slow recovery. I could scarcely stomach the treats Mom was bringing along from home, let alone the sponge-like hospital food, so my nutrients were derived chiefly from that big milky bag, spiked into my arm. Until I could eat, there would be no talk of me going home. And so I lay there for a week, worrying, thinking about what had happened over the past year and a half, and trying to find some peace among the conflicting opinions that jostled for authenticity in my head.

Lying there, I began to realise – perhaps for the first time – that medicine was by no means an exact science with clear and absolute solutions. It was, at best, a game of educated guesswork around the perplexing workings inside the mysterious human body. At moments I contemplated the mistakes that might have been made. How much faster might I have recovered without nine months of chemotherapy further weakening my immune system? What had a year of intense morphine addiction done to my body?

I felt flashes of rage, not so much for the possible errors, but for the lack of holistic perspectives among the experts I'd been consulting. Of course, I'd come across information that morphine was perfectly safe – I'd heard it from the consultants at Hospice, from my haematologist, in brochures I'd picked up at the oncology centre – and from a whole host of experts in dealing with people who were likely to be dying. And in that context of extreme suffering and poor prognoses, morphine is probably as safe as anything else. But what was safe? Was chemotherapy itself safe? Certainly not, but was dying of cancer any safer?

And so, as I lay there figuring, it became apparent to me that each expert worked within his or her own little specialised field, doing their best to deal with the crises they were faced with – regardless, to some degree, of the side effects on other parts of the body, and leaving those to someone else to deal with. And the fact that all these organs needed to function at the same time within a single human body was ultimately no one's responsibility but my own.

There was no point in delving into the past – no matter how severe the consequences had been. What was the sense in rage or retribution? Right then, I needed to heal, and the anger would only corrode me – I needed to acknowledge it, but if I wanted to get better I would need to let go of it. Whoever had acted had done so within the best of their abilities and with my best interests at heart. And, like all of us, they were fallible.

After all, here was a deadly virus that was barely twenty years old. Ten years ago, my chances of making it this far would have been extremely slim. Despite money, support and current expertise, so early into its treatment, there were as few clear facts about Aids as there was any surety of a drug cocktail that would turn a terminal illness into a chronic, manageable disease. With such a drastically compromised immune system, the innocuous-sounding phrase 'opportunistic infections' carried with it an unimaginable scope of complications. And there was only so much a body could take at one time. With such an endless array of guesses, opinions and treatments surrounding me, the best I could hope for was to put myself in the hands of the one I believed to be the most knowledgeable and available expert – and hope.

At around 11 p.m. that night, Quentin called and asked if I was I up for a pop-in. I told the nurses my older brother was on his way, and they turned a kind blind eye to any Visiting Hours drama. Quen arrived and I lit a ciggie. The nurses had long stopped fighting with me. A couple of times they had caught me in the act, and simply requested that I not burn the place down – a fair request given my prostrate position, analgesic haze and the badly positioned saucer of an ashtray in the drawer of the bedside pedestal. I sure hoped I wouldn't – it would be a shame to go down in a hospital blaze after all this. 'D'you know what I'd kill for?' I asked Quen, half-joking. 'A joint.'

'Well, actually,' he smiled mischievously, 'I happen to have a roach in the car. With everything else you're on, I don't think a little harmless marijuana would do you any major damage.' And so, a few moments later, we respectfully closed the door, opened the windows and fogged up the ward with the thick, heavy stench of dagga smoke as a collection of Bob Marley remixes spun away appropriately on the stereo.

We chatted. Kept it normal and day to day, as if I wasn't half-dying as I lay there. Quen yawned, and I thanked him and kissed him goodnight. And I lay there, a little trippy, drifting into semi-consciousness, playing out the John Martyn CD until that last beautiful song. I was beginning to understand the most obvious and perplexing of human riddles – that the *end* that we placed so much importance on didn't actually matter at all, because it was the end – finished. What mattered were the beginnings – everything the weather had been so blessed as to blow into my life and everything that happened along the way.

TRIAL AND ERROR

I WAS DISCHARGED AFTER A week, better, but by no means recovered. The new antibiotics and painkillers I was on were playing havoc with my stomach. Sometimes I'd start bloating in the afternoon, sometimes in the early evening. I was at home, but so uncomfortable most of the time, all I could do was lie back, wasting away the hours, with my bony knee raised. It was often impossible to get hold of Dr S. At one point I waited a week before I finally got hold of him. This left all of us in a state of desperate frustration. What was the point of being in the hands of the best specialist in town, if he remained so infuriatingly inaccessible?

A couple of times, the cramps became so unbearable again that I was rushed to casualty for a drip. Because my damaged stomach was not responding to oral painkillers, the only possible relief was intravenous. I felt awful, asking Mom to rush me to casualty at 2 a.m. on a Sunday morning, but it did allow me sufficient relief to fall asleep on the way home.

We checked for infection in the stomach but the tests came back clear. The other possibility, Dr S explained, when I finally got through to his cellphone, was that I was reacting badly to the medication. Now all that was required was to figure out of which of the sixty tablets I was swallowing each day was causing the drama. We would do this through a tedious process of elimination – looking for signs of improvement and then reintroducing the possible troublemakers one by one. At best it would require a simple change of antibiotics; worse, it would entail the tricky process of altering the anti-retrovirals that had been successfully keeping the virus undetectable in my body for the past year and a half. Now, more than ever, it seemed like a scarily amateur game of trial and error.

I stopped taking two of the antibiotics for a couple of days, and began to notice an improvement. It was absolute heaven to feel a flat gut and have nothing but excruciating foot pain to contend with. But I awoke the following morning with a high fever. I tried in vain to contact Dr S. The following day the fever was higher and I finally got hold of him. In the absence of the antibiotics, the TB was spinning out of control. Tentatively we would need to introduce some new antibiotics, and, of course, there were only so many options available. One of them was thalidomide. As horrific as this sounded, I wasn't the least bit perturbed. I'd tried antidepressant medication for my feet at one stage, and anti-schizophrenic medication for some chronic chemo-induced bouts of hiccoughs. Medicines, I'd discovered, had some quite useful side effects.

And so I started the new medications. The fevers stopped, but by the following evening I had begun to bloat again. The diarrhoea had returned with a vengeance. I was worried, but Dr S had expressed in his usual calming manner that 'these tummy things take a while to sort out' – words that had an eerily familiar ring to me.

Unable to digest and hold my food, and with a damaged stomach lining, I couldn't expect much from my medications. I wasn't sure whether the escalating pain in my feet had to do with the painkillers that weren't making it into my bloodstream or the fact that nothing could hope to compare with the potency of the morphine. That afternoon a chunk of tooth fell out of the back of my mouth.

SHADOWS

I SAW THE DENTIST THE following day. He managed to patch up my back right molar with cement, but cautioned me that the tooth would require root canal treatment. He wasn't sure that I was up to it in my current state. Another option was extraction, but he was doubtful about my healing abilities, and wary of the further antibiotics this would require. 'There are lots of cavities in your mouth,' he observed cursorily. 'But I don't want to do anything too invasive right now. We're going to have to deal with them in the New Year.'

I went home, glum at the prospect of root canal and fearful of what other dramas might be lurking inside my mouth. A few hours later, the last surviving wall of that same tooth collapsed, leaving only a couple of shards poking through the gum. As opposed as the dentist was to extractions in general, in this case he felt it was the best option, so I was booked in for surgery.

The extraction was completely painless. The surgeon was gentle, preparing me in advance for any discomfort I might feel. In six minutes, he managed to slice open my gums and extract the last rotten bits of root and stitch me up. Dad drove me back from the surgery, numb but painless.

About four days later I began feeling some pain on the other side of my mouth. I couldn't figure out whether it was top or bottom. And with all the painkillers I was on, I couldn't tell how serious it might be, but with everything I was going through I kind of hoped this would just go away on its own. It didn't. And so, the next morning, I was back in the dentist's chair for an X-ray. 'Let's just deal with what we need to right now,' I pleaded. 'I'm going through a hell of a lot right now and I don't think I could handle much more drama.'

He had always been a very calm and reassuring man, but when he stepped back into the room a short while later, he was beside himself, wiping his brow in exasperation. 'Okay, how bad can it be?' I asked.

'Very bad,' he said. 'Very, very bad. I know you don't want to go into all of this right now, but I have to show you what is happening.' He held the X-ray up to the light. 'You see these shadows between the teeth. Every single one of these teeth is severely decayed. They're all going to need root work.'

'But what happened? Was it the medication?'

'Yes, I suspect it was. I X-rayed your mouth eighteen months ago and your teeth were all in great shape. Now …' He emitted a weak, trembling sigh. 'Does that sound express how I feel?'

'Are we talking dentures?'

'Yes,' he said gravely. 'Quite possibly.'

I was devastated. He had only X-rayed one section of my mouth, but it seemed likely that the scenario was similarly grim all over. I had sensed things happening in my mouth over the past year, I'd felt cracks at the gum-line with my tongue and there seemed to be gaps widening between the teeth, but with everything I was going through at the time, I didn't have the strength to go for a dental check-up. I remembered seeing something in a brochure at the cancer clinic about how chemotherapy affects the teeth, and I had taken care to brush and floss regularly, but no one had mentioned the slightest possibility of anything this drastic occurring.

The following Monday, a full mouth X-ray at the root canal specialist confirmed my unspoken fears. The rot was equally dire throughout. 'We need to deal with this,' the specialist said. 'And sooner rather than later. It's bad timing, unfortunately. Everyone is closing for Christmas.

In the meanwhile, I suggest you deal with it symptomatically. Then, in January, when the labs open, we will get impressions taken and start having the dentures made. No, we can't do implants. They won't take with all the medication you're on. I think we should do the back lot first so that you can get used to them.'

'Them?'

'The dentures.'

'And the front?'

'We'll see, but it will probably be the front as well.'

* * *

Somehow, it seems tooth decay is always associated with guilt, but the specialist confirmed that both my oral hygiene and my bones were good; the rot had seeped in from the gums, between the teeth. I couldn't have felt it or seen it. It had happened from the inside from some substance that had been put into my body. Right then, I should have felt rage, but I didn't, and that worried me. Had I become so acquiescent to the toll of this disease that I couldn't even access my emotions? Had I become so submissive it had rendered me impotent?

I called my various doctors with the news, but none of them seemed willing to take any responsibility. They'd never heard of anything quite so drastic, they claimed. Was it the chemo? No one was sure, but it seemed likely, or, failing that, a combination of that and the antibiotics and the HIV. My head was reeling. Who knows? If I'd been warned about this, was there anything I could have done to stop it? And, even if there was, would I have had the strength to handle all the dreadful drilling and pulling required? If it was the chemo, and if the chemo had really been unnecessary, then this consequence seemed all the more cruel. I was entitled to anger, or at the very least, to an explanation. I dialled the oncologist's office and spoke with the nurse.

'Oh, Adam, I'm so sorry to hear that,' she said.

'Yeah, well, I'm not phoning to blame anyone,' I said meekly. 'But I do think it's something you should warn future patients about.'

'Oh, I really am sorry,' she repeated, and she meant it, but like everyone else, she was non-committal. 'Shall I get the doctor to call you?'

'Yeah, well, tell him about it. Tell him he can call me about it if he wants to.'

He didn't.

ENDURANCE

It took a good few days to adjust to this devastating news. Dentures at thirty-five. It seemed like a bad joke. I sat gloomily imagining a Last Supper of sirloin steak before they yanked the whole rotten lot out of me. The glass at the side of the bed, with the clappers smiling in it. How embarrassingly premature. I wondered if anyone would ever kiss me again. And I wondered if there wasn't any other possible course of action. I went for two further opinions, but they couldn't tell me anything more positive. And so, slowly, I began to get used to it. There were plenty of people hopping around the planet without their own teeth, leading full and happy lives, and I was soon to join them.

Meanwhile, the rest of my health complaints were by no means resolved. I wasn't rushing to the hospital for intravenous relief every night, but my stomach remained extremely sensitive, bloating more on some days and less on others. There were cramps sometimes in the mornings, but I knew the next step in Dr S's process would be to change my anti-retrovirals and I didn't want that. It wasn't getting worse; it appeared to be an uncomfortable condition, which would hopefully improve once I was through with some of my TB medication in a few months. So I decided to live with it. The bloating was certainly exacerbated if I ate the wrong sorts of foods, so I experimented with different ways of eating. Foods that had previously seemed totally innocuous, I now inspected with anxious trepidation before I put them into my mouth. So many things I had once taken so for granted had now become delicate and complicated.

Without the morphine, my foot pain was much harder to manage. While previously I had always got through a passable day and waited with dread for the pain to worsen in the evening, now the pain could worsen at any time of the day, sometimes all day. I experimented with various painkillers, but the symptoms remained erratic. I went for a spinal injection that Dr S had said would offer a probability of full or partial relief. Dr D had been dubious.

The next afternoon, yet another specialist pushed a needle into the tissue next to my spine. 'Did it work?' he asked.

After a year and half of agony, how on earth could I conceive of the pain vanishing in an instant? 'I don't know,' I said. 'My feet feel different. I don't know if they feel better, but they feel different.'

I so desperately wanted it to work that for the next couple of days, I thought it might have made some difference. But it hadn't. And so, for the time being, I lived with the pain.

THE WORLD

It was 1 December, World Aids Day. A couple of people SMSed me to mark its importance, but I still didn't feel part of the big wide world of Aids. From the beginning, I had lived in my own tiny world of this disease. There were a couple of documentaries on TV and Dad was watching them. At first he called out to tell me, but then he came in and said maybe I didn't want to watch. There were awful shots of emaciated people in hospital and it might get me down, he said. But that got me watching.

The programme I watched was brilliant. It sketched out the magnitude of the disease and how ill-equipped the world is to deal with such a pandemic. It showed how apocalyptic the statistics are. If just 5 per cent of India's population became infected, that would mean 50 million people would need treatment. It showed a hospital there, where women, infected by their husbands, shunned and thrown out of their households, had come to wait for drugs. Sick as they were, they took eight-hour shifts, sharing beds between three of them.

The film showed a beautiful young girl from Uganda, who had been orphaned at twelve, and had been flown to Washington to address the Vice-President. Her gleaming smile and spirit were the epitome of hope. It was impossible not to be moved by the power of her spirit, in spite of everything she had suffered. If there was any plea for a better world with a better future, she was it. But she had died, at twenty-one, of meningitis. I was moved to tears, and yet it all still seemed so very far away.

MY WORLD

BACK IN JOHANNESBURG, I was managing a few sedentary hours each day and then resorting to a sofa with my feet propped up on some pillows to drain the swelling and ease the pain. But most of the time either my stomach was too bloated or my feet were too sore to sit up. It was just as well the paper had folded when it did, because I was able to be less and less productive. And because my mood was always so much more robust when I had managed a decent amount of work during the day, my spirit had begun to weaken. My sense of purpose was threatened. If I couldn't even write, then what the hell was I doing?

At times, I'd lie there evaluating the quality of my existence. All the while, I had believed that I was through the worst and that it was simply a matter of patience before things improved dramatically. But recent events had changed that. I had suffered a tremendous setback, and now I found myself as disabled, in more pain and with more complications to worry about than I'd had during the darkest moments of 2004. For me, and for the few people who remained committed to seeing me better, this whole affair was taking dramatically longer than we'd ever imagined.

The goalposts had shifted as the journey progressed. At first I'd thought, get on the pills and soon life will be back to normal. Then a few months passed. Then a year. And, with each blow, we had all silently digested the information and carried on, without acknowledging the slightest waning of hope. But now I was halfway into another year, and whatever 'normal' was seemed further away than ever. I was beginning to grasp that 'normal' might never be normal again.

The exhausting process of recovery had taken its toll on the people around me. For the past eighteen months, Mom had rarely spent a few hours beyond a couple of kilometres' radius, making sure I was always adequately supplied with nutrition and good cheer and that we were never in danger of running short of pills. That the blasted bucket, a bottle of water, the humidifier, cigarettes and the various emergency medications were all safely at my bedside when she dimmed the lights at curfew time. Dad, too, had made himself available to take me to doctor's appointments, help me with errands and come and chat with me when I was feeling down. By the end of 2004, my parents were both physically and emotionally fatigued.

It was rare that we dared discuss or even contemplate the bigger picture, but occasionally I just burst. I told them how guilty I felt, having become such a huge financial strain and emotional burden to them, and they reassured me that they weren't going short, and that for them, there could not have been any other choice. 'I never imagined what an immense and tedious drama this would turn out to be,' I expressed. And then Dad said something blatantly obvious that had never struck me before. 'Of course it is,' he said. 'It's the worst thing that's ever happened to you. Even for me – it's the worst thing that's happened in my life.'

I was humbled by how totally unconditional their support had been. A younger, less mature me would have surely given up on someone after such an unreasonably long period.

The situation with my friends was not as simple as with my folks. Many people in my life had disappeared. There had been waves of departures. A few close friends, quite unable to confront any degree of sickness or mortality, had vanished as soon as I'd moved to my parents' house, and I hadn't laid eyes on them since. Then, as the months dragged on, others had begun calling less frequently – promising visits that never happened and then staying away, paralysed by guilt. Others had simply carried on with their lives, following paths that took them to different places. They continued to phone and e-mail dutifully, but I missed them terribly – especially Kate.

With the amount I got out and mingled, the chances of me meeting new people were slim, and so my world had shrunk vastly. My core of friends had dwindled to a small, committed group, who never failed to amaze and inspire me with the extent of their stamina and dedication. But after my recent setback, even they were taking strain.

A few people had come to see me in hospital, but I was so bewildered and uncomfortable, I failed to recognise the effect it had on them, seeing me in such a miserable state. Although no one dared express anything but optimism, privately, the people who loved me were devastated by recent events. Like me, they had taken it for granted that there would be a consistent improvement. Excruciatingly slow as that process was proving to be, they had needed to believe, above all else, that there would be a happy ending to this saga, or at the very least a manageable one. Now none of that seemed certain. The whole eventuality of recovery hung in the balance. Our little world had been shaken, and without my knowledge, my friends and family were all struggling deeply with this emotionally.

One Saturday morning, Alex called and said she'd meet me for coffee. Zingi, a colleague who had moved into my house as a new tenant while I was in hospital, came along, and we sat down brightly to croissants and cappuccinos. But within moments the conversation felt very strained. We had all recently lost our jobs, so that was an obvious reason for our vulnerability, but each time Alex tried to explain where she was at, I misunderstood her.

'I'm very emotional at the moment,' she expressed.

'I know, Al,' I said, hoping to reassure her. 'But you're underestimating your strength. I know you'll be able to get through this.'

'No, Addie, you're not getting me,' she said. She was becoming tearful, frustrated. I so wanted to understand her, but with each attempt at connection, we seemed more and more doomed to failure. We trembled our way through the cappuccinos.

'I know you're emotional, Al,' I said. 'But you'll handle it.'

'You just don't get it, Addie!' she cried. 'It's you! I'm emotional about you! Visiting you in hospital and seeing you like that – you don't know what it did to me. All this time you were supposed to be getting better, but you haven't been. You haven't been putting on weight, you can hardly walk and we've all just carried on as if everything is merrily improving but it isn't. I miss our friendship, Addie – the way it used to be. I miss just hanging out and smoking a joint or going out wherever and whenever we wanted to. But it's not like that any more. And it's upsetting me.'

I was silent. Of course nothing I could say could ease her pain – because my suffering was the cause of it. So much of what had just exploded all over the café's breakfast table was what we had all been feeling for so long, and yet, nobody had had the balls to express it. For so many years, this had been the fundament of our friendship – a willingness to plough the depths of emotion, no matter how intense. While others shied away from expressing those feelings, for us there had never been anything too messy or dramatic to explore, and yet, some things had still slipped by unspoken. 'I know,' I said. 'It's just taking so fucking long. Who ever dreamt anything would take this long?'

'That's not it,' she despaired. 'I'll be there. If you're sick like this for ten years, I'll be there. I just need you to understand how upset I'm feeling. How I'm feeling about you.'

There was nothing more to be said. We finished our cappuccinos awkwardly and the mood improved. We all spent the day together. We got stoned and laughed and felt lighter, but somewhere beneath the surface, everyone felt the gravity of what had finally been said. The events of the past two months had shaken our world, all over again, and despite the brave smiles and the unflinching displays of hope, again, we were facing the fear that I just might not get better.

Even then, I don't think I dared grasp the depth of Alex's feelings for me. Despite the enormous pressures she was under, she had remained at my side, through every terrifying turn in this journey, through each sickening hospital stay, through each moment that had seemed it might be the last. Only she knew me well enough to listen and talk me through the emotional complexities of this safari. If, at times, I failed to acknowledge that in this memoir, it was for two reasons: Firstly, I simply could not comprehend that anyone, apart from my family, could care so very much about me, and that the prospect of my not being here one day might leave such a great hole in someone else's life. Never before had I encountered such overwhelming compassion. But more than that, I suspect, our connection had always been so vast, so deep and so intuitive that I struggled to separate her existence from my own. If Alex vanished from this text at times, it was because she was part of me. She was inside my fingers as I typed. Inside my pain, my fear, even my loneliness.

A week later, she played me a song by Maxwell that

had brought her to tears a few nights previously. I listened to the sweet, soulful harmonies until the song reached its chorus, and, finally, I understood what Alex had been so devastated by. Maxwell sang it and we both grasped all the fear and sadness so perfectly contained in his masterful lingering falsetto. 'You and I were supposed to grow old.'

INVISIBLE

OVER THE PAST COUPLE of months, I'd been working on a novel. With one book at the printers and this one banished from my mind, the new book was fulfilling a great part of my need to feel purposeful. For the first time in my life, I felt able to write fiction. I believed in the characters I was creating and couldn't wait to get back to the keyboard and explore the drama that was evolving among them. Even in hospital, I'd sit on the edge of my bed, hurriedly typing away and immersing myself in a thrilling fictitious world. But now, as my ability to sit up and work diminished, my interest began to flag. The few times I managed to sit at a desk, I stared at a blank screen, lost and paralysed. As often happens, I lost faith in the manuscript and had no idea where to take it next.

This terrified me. I had a couple of freelance commitments pending, but nothing that would truly satiate my hunger for purpose. As I battled with the various unpredictable pains of teeth and tummy and feet, my ability to concentrate grew weaker. I'd pick up a book and read a few pages, before dismissing it as inconsequential. As the days passed, I struggled to find meaning in anything.

Late one afternoon, Mom was rushing to the pharmacy to replenish some of my drugs and I decided to go with her. I was looking grim at the time, pale and skinny and bloated, and sporting a botched home hair-dye experiment to boot. I had hoped that 'Golden Blonde' might have the same uplifting effect as the mirrored shoe, but the result had been a frightening ginger. Distraught, I pinned my hopes on a pack of 'Sunny Blonde' that Mom had in the house, but that had resulted in a disappointing crown of glistening copper. Desperate, I hobbled out and bought a pack of 'Pale Blonde', but with everything my poor locks had suffered in the past two days, I was left, inevitably I suppose, with a dull beige that did as little for my sallow, patchy complexion as it did for my self-esteem. Undaunted, I made my way to the mall with Mom, and braved a hobble around the bookshop.

It had happened a few times when I'd ventured out – I'd encounter faces I remembered. Sometimes, if I was feeling vulnerable, I'd hide behind a pillar, too weary for confrontation or explanation. And today was one of those days. I spotted someone I'd known fairly well, and he looked straight through me. Maybe he didn't recognise fifteen kilograms less of me. Or maybe he did, but didn't know what to say to someone so evidently unwell. If I was frightened to look in the mirror at times, I could understand his trepidation. Terrified of registering pity in his eyes, I kept my distance and when, as fate would have it, we arrived at the checkout counter together, I kept my gaze in the middle distance.

It was not the first time I had felt invisible. Healthy-looking HIV-positive people appeared on TV, bravely declaring their status, but where were the sick ones? Sure, I'd seen them in documentaries – skeletons, rolled up in blankets in remote huts or craning out their emaciated arms for a handshake on a celebrity hospital round, but I never saw them in the supermarket or at restaurants. Burdened by stigmas and fear, Aids had hidden itself. All over again, I found myself locked in a closet.

It was insane. The figures said one in eight or one in five South Africans were HIV-positive, but most of the time I felt as though I was the only person in the world with Aids. Aside from a rare phone call from one sick friend and two uplifting visits from someone who had conquered the worst and was managing this disease sufficiently to live some kind of full life, my experience of Aids had been a lonely one. And as much as the angels around me tried to ease my discomfort or bolster my hopes at recovery, I yearned for some sense of camaraderie. It was all sympathy and no empathy.

I'd thought of joining a support group, but Dr S had warned me about the potentially negative elements within such groups, and how they might affect my so-called 'indomitable spirit'. But sometimes I didn't feel all that indomitable. I was frightened. I was worried about the future, if there even was such a thing.

Gradually, the contact I'd had with the hipsters on the club scene had whittled down to the odd misdirected SMS, simply because my name was at the top of an alphabetical list and prone to the odd unintentional call. I heard phones chafing in pockets. Engines running. Once, at 6 a.m., I was rudely invited to eavesdrop on an arbitrary argument between some old friends who had stayed up all night. I heard them ragging one another in Afrikaans for thirty seconds, coming down from something, I guess, just as I was staggering to the sofa to take my morning painkillers. Our lives, which had once been so similar, now seemed irreconcilably different.

Seeing as I spent most of my time at home, and hadn't been out in the evening for a year and a half, I guess some of those people wondered where I was. Back in New York perhaps. Or settled down cosily with someone, raising Dalmatians. Or dead. Others, I suppose, had simply carried on with their lives and forgotten me.

ALONE

It was that frightening time of year, when everyone was going off on their Christmas holidays. Despite the inconvenient timing of my precarious health, the pressures of a joyous festive season were looming. Dad had headed down to Cape Town for a break, and I wanted Mom to join him. Previously, they had taken their holidays in shifts, but I knew how crucial it was that they spend some real time together – away from the constant nursing requirements of their dependent thirty-five-year-old toddler. Mom was scheduled to leave on the 22nd, but somewhere in the back of my mouth, another drama was erupting and I was still clearly too vulnerable to be left alone. So Mom postponed for a week.

We headed for the dentist. 'Right-hand side,' I said.

'Top or bottom?'

'I'm not sure.'

He tapped a series of eight teeth to see which one was causing the pain, but none felt any different from the others. He took a look inside. 'It could be any of them,' he said, exasperated. 'They're all decayed. But I've got a hunch it's tooth 16.' He tapped 16. It felt no different. 'Yes,' I lied. 'That's the tooth.' He called the specialist who was on standby for the season and arranged for an extraction the following morning.

That evening, as the pain set in, I did my best to locate the tooth, but I couldn't. The next morning, I met with a brusque butcher, who took a brief glance at my X-rays and proposed getting me into a clinic, knocking me out and yanking the whole back lot out immediately. 'You'll be on soft foods for a month or so with the dentures in any case,' he snapped. 'So you might as well just get used to it. In the meanwhile, your gums will heal and they can make the dentures.'

The idea of an imminent return to hospital seemed frightful. With my stomach and my weight just beginning to recover, the prospect of further antibiotics and a month of compromised nutrition seemed worse. 'I can remove that tooth, but I can't offer you any guarantee that it's the right one,' he said. 'They're all shot.' His waiting room was full and he needed an answer immediately. 'What's it going to be?'

It felt like Russian roulette, only instead of a single loaded cartridge, the barrel was full, but for a single blank.

'Tooth Sixteen,' I said. The odds were eight to one, but I took my chances. The tooth was a mess. The crown was almost totally decayed and crumbled under the immense pressure of the forceps. Eventually, he produced the chunky, bloody root of a molar and dropped it, clink, into a tin dish. I felt weak and brutalised – as though I'd been bashed over the head, and I headed home, hoping to God Sixteen had been my lottery ticket.

* * *

And so Mom was leaving. I had become so dependent on her that the prospect of her absence for a couple of weeks truly frightened me, but I was determined that if my condition was stable, she should go. I kept my fears to myself, and we prepared a car-load of provisions for the journey to my house. Zingi would be around some of the time and Mary would be available to help me, and yet, deep down, I was terrified at the prospect of being abandoned in a crisis. As Mom drove me home, I wished her well, hoping the break would offer her some of the replenishment she deserved. We carted the provisions into my house, I hugged her goodbye and she left. And, standing there, alone in my bedroom, at thirty-five years old, I burst into tears.

ZINGI

I WAS DELIGHTED THAT ZINGI had moved in. He was insightful, way beyond his twenty-five years, and compassionate, but he had a sufficiently hectic schedule to be immersed in his own life. It seemed a perfect balance – he was helpful, but not so attentive that I felt as if I had become his responsibility. The evening I moved back home, we sat down and talked. As I was soon to learn, we would never lack for drama.

In two hours, he informed me, his long-time, on-off, deepest-ever love was arriving from England. This visit would determine for him whether or not, regardless of geography, this relationship was worth fighting for. It felt strange discussing someone else's love life, when my own was currently so utterly barren. But I felt quite at peace with that. This was not a time for intimacy. The thought of allowing anyone within close physical proximity of my fragile body frightened the shit out of me. Right then, I simply needed to love and nurture myself.

The following morning, Zingi and I had coffee. From the expression on his face, I knew that the previous night's connection had been intense. And, as he spoke, I knew instinctively what he was about to tell me. The long-awaited reunion had been complicated by some perplexing news. A couple of months ago, Zingi's beau – the one out of so many current options that he ultimately wanted to make a serious go of it with – had tested HIV-positive. He was not yet on medication, but his cell count was between 200 and 250 and he was visibly thinner.

Zingi was no stranger to HIV. Though he was negative, his ex-lover had been positive for more than a decade and was a prominent Aids activist. Many of his friends were involved in prevention or monitoring programmes. And here he was, living with me, going through the rigours of my screaming feet, angry teeth and inflatable stomach. 'I don't even understand why they are talking about prevention any more,' he said. 'It doesn't make any sense to me. 'Cos it's closing in on me. It's everywhere. It's in all the people I love.'

2005

IT WAS THE 31ST OF DECEMBER – the most terrifying day of the year. The day when one is riddled with anxiety about the passage into a new chapter. Could it ever live up to its immense expectations? Would it rise to heights of joyous celebration? Or would it sink to the depths of misery? No matter how much I'd battled through, the thought of lying in my bed, with my pain as my only companion, as the clock ticked into 2005 was too tragic to contemplate. I knew this passage was simply another journey from light into darkness and back into light, another one of 365 million days in the history of histories, and yet I could not escape the immense significance that this single night always carried with it.

As per tradition, my dear friends Ren and Teri had invited me to dinner at their house, but I was worried about my stamina levels. My foot pain had scarcely been bearable in the evenings, and I was worried about writhing in pain in public and spoiling the celebratory mood. And as daunted as I was by the loneliest night of the year, a part of me would far rather have been comfortable in bed. I told Ren and Teri I'd play it by ear.

* * *

The afternoon went well, sorting through old CDs and playing favourite songs with Zingi. Come six o'clock, I felt strong. I changed out of my standard loose-fitting patient's gear into a tighter, glitzier outfit for the occasion. It was the first time I'd braved leaving the house after dark since Alex's birthday party in July.

The evening that followed was utterly precious. It was spent with a small, intimate group of people. The company was so delightful, I required no more stimulation than two glasses of water the entire evening. Ren had prepared a feast of fresh trout, stuffed with Asian spices, roasted lightly on the fire, combined with the macrobiotic delights of marinated tofu and buckwheat noodles. My feet rose impeccably to the occasion, allowing me to stay sedentary for most of the evening. I was so encouraged that I even considered joining them all on their adventure to an underground rave downtown, but at 10:30 I yawned, and asked Teri to take me home. The evening had been so rich and beautiful, I felt totally sated.

I kissed Zingi goodnight on his way out, and crawled happily into bed at 11. And by the annual moment of unsurpassable drama, I was curled up in bed, in a blissfully oblivious zzz.

180 DEGREES

AND SO ANOTHER YEAR had passed. There seemed something incredibly fatalistic in the way my life had changed. In so many ways, it had taken an 180-degree turn. Memories flashed through my head like a slide show. New York, Marrakech, Zanzibar, Madagascar, Borneo, São Paulo, Miami, Abidjan, Mombasa, Amsterdam, Lima, London – a hundred places perhaps, scattered all over the planet. It was almost inconceivable that for the past year and a half, I had been confined within a safe, manageable radius of a few kilometres, comprising my own home, my parents' home, various medical facilities and the occasional stumble into a shopping mall.

I remembered another kind of existence. Screeching up to my friends' houses and hustling them out of bed on a Wednesday, proclaiming 'Klein Saterdag', or little Saturday. Who cared if anyone else knew it wasn't really weekend? We were out there, causing delicious havoc in any godforsaken place that was open.

I remember New York. Going out drinking every night, until closing time at 4 a.m. I remember the insane weekly routine. Mondays – Sabor Latino at the Monster, which translated as Latin Flavour, and somewhere around 2 a.m. the flava began to diffuse, as the dance floor pulsed with Cuban beats. Then only the most skilled *son* dancers would take over, storming and spinning the place into a sweat-drenched frenzy.

I remember Flashback Tuesdays, when disco tracks would come whizzing out of the eighties, and I'd transform myself, at whim, on the dance floor, stripping down to my underwear and slipping into a full-length white lycra gown that I'd scrunched niftily into my goatskin bag.

Wednesdays – when we'd trawl the Chelsea bars,

catching a half-hour of whichever drag queen was hosting some insane game show. Thursdays – for all the dark avant-garde drama at The Cock in the East Village.

On one occasion, I recall, The Cock was hosting its weekly talent contest, 'Foxy'. The goal was to discover the foxiest person in New York. I witnessed many winners, but somehow the one that has stayed with me was a heterosexual Filipina woman in her fifties, who stripped and prostrated herself to perform Michael Jackson's 'Moonwalk'. The edgy gay crowd had never seen anything like this, and Jackie Beat, the event's larger than life MC, summed up the general astonishment perfectly when she rolled her eyes and muttered dryly, 'Gotta love it!'

And Fridays – tossing down another ten Coronas and checking out the universe of talent at Splash. Come Saturday, it would probably be some obscure bar, dodging the amateurs who had bridged or tunnelled their way into Manhattan from Queens or New Jersey. Then Sundays – I can't even remember the name of the club. I just remember Hip Hop honeys in bling and fake leopard skin and real fur, and trippy club kids parading around in God only knows what until deep into Monday morning, when a few hours' sleep and a wardrobe check would give me sufficient nerve to start the whole cycle again.

I was insatiable. I was out there, looking for something or someone. Finding them. Losing them. Losing it. Collecting memories, perhaps, in preparation for the immense transformation that lay ahead of me.

Indeed, for the past year and half, my immobility at night has imposed such a rigorous curfew on my existence that I have ventured but twice beyond the safety of home after sunset. I have waited nightly for 10.15 p.m., when the lights are dimmed and the bleep, bleep, bleep of the alarm system has imprisoned me in my teenage bedroom. Is it possible that the same person could live such vastly opposite lives?

Of course it is. For, as I am learning, our capacity for adaptation is way beyond our imagination. Once we have stepped over the threshold of fear, our ability to change is immeasurable. What had once seemed so indispensable had now become blissfully irrelevant. Hungers that had driven me over the cliffs of desire had now vanished so completely I could scarcely remember what they felt like. Emotions that had ruled my existence now ceased to exist, and new ones that I had never imagined had taken their place. Inevitably, in more ways than I would ever have imagined, Aids had changed me.

THIRTY-SIX

THE FOLLOWING SUNDAY WAS my birthday. Although there was no certainty of any more such days, I had survived another year, and from sunrise to sunset, 9 January 2005 was a day full of blessings. I spent it surrounded by people I love, spoilt with precious gifts, and gorged blissfully on my favourite pink and orange pineapple pudding from my Aunty Shirley.

God knows why perhaps, but everything was pink and orange that day. Serendipitously, almost everyone just happened to pitch up in my favourite colours. They matched the tablecloth and the flower arrangements and the wrapping paper, and the colourful symbolism filled my house and my soul. Pink for love and orange for happiness. Come evening, I was exhausted and I collapsed into bed feeling rich and full.

    Another year on this planet. And each moment a bonus.

PART THREE

STEPHEN'S GIFT

12 January 2005

For weeks, there had been promises of a visit from a guy called Stephen. Mom knew him from her work and we knew he was an Aids survivor. Right in the beginning, he'd tried to get me an appointment with Dr S, but somehow it hadn't happened. I knew he still suffered horrible neuropathy, but that he ran around on those feet from morning to night and made himself a damn good living. Every now and then I'd wrench out some sketchy, second-hand information on pain management. 'Prop the feet up on a pillow at night so the swelling can drain out of them.' But what about during the day? 'Rub tea tree oil on them.' But how much?

With all the eerie silence around me, I had little idea how much personal territory Stephen would be willing to reveal. I knew he'd been very close to death at one point, at a time when Aids was such an unspeakable disease he'd left the country for six months to be treated in distant privacy. I knew he'd gradually become more open about his experience, but how open? There were so many questions I wanted to ask someone who'd been there and was still here. But Stephen was busy. Stephen was in New York or London. So I waited patiently for my promised appointment of hope, until, one evening, Stephen came bounding into my parents' living room, in classic black and white, and sat himself down beside me, still yakking on his cellphone.

Within the next few minutes it became clear that Stephen had come here for a reason, and that in his own, wickedly amusing way, he was going to tell me everything my ears needed to hear, whether I wanted to listen or not.

'Now listen to me,' he began, prodding me on the knee. 'I want you to understand something: You don't die from this any more. Not if you have money. Not if you're in a First World country, with First World medicine. Do you hear what I'm saying? *You don't die from this.*'

The cellphone chirped. 'Hello ... No, not right now. I'll call you back. Give me half an hour.'

It was clear that Stephen had not had reason to worry about money in the course of his illness, but that he'd had serious reason to worry about his life. Back in the dark days of 1996, his six foot one frame had wasted down to a terrifying thirty-nine kilos. He had been hospitalised for a year and a half. His neuropathy had affected his arm so badly he had spent months with it in a sling. 'Did you ever have Kaposi's?' I asked.

'No,' he smiled in amazement. 'That was the one thing I didn't get. I got everything else. You name it, I had it. Two round-the-clock nurses for months. And they hated me in that hospital. I was a nightmare. Always demanding another doctor. Another opinion. Until, eventually, one of my specialists came to me and said, "Stephen. You can't have eight doctors. You aren't going to get better like this. It's just too many."'

The phone chirped again. 'Hello, Mrs Pest! ... No, don't do anything in the meantime. I'll be there at nine o'clock tomorrow morning. Okay? Mrs Pest, goodbye.' He pushed the phone a few centimetres away. 'These clients!' he despaired, throwing his hands to the ceiling. 'Did you hear what I call her? If these people don't stop bothering me, I swear I'm going to switch this thing off.' But he didn't. He turned, and looked me right in the eyes. 'I don't know what it was,' he said quietly. 'But somehow, somewhere, there was something. Not even me. Some *thing*. Something wanted me to live. And you've got to find that something. Because that's what's going to get you through.'

'What was your cell count?' I asked.

'Two,' he replied, and I slapped him a high five.

'What was your viral load?'

'Billions!' he exclaimed. 'The figure was so high, they couldn't measure it.'

It was so deeply reassuring for me to hear someone who looked so miraculously normal speaking these words – the same words that had looped endlessly in the prison of my mind. To know that my pain had also been someone else's pain. That my fear had been someone else's fear. To know that, through it all, I had not been so utterly alone.

Stephen sipped on some mineral water and bummed a cigarette. 'Do me one favour,' he beseeched. 'Don't give up on Dr S. If he tells you to eat gravel from the street, then you do it. I know he's difficult, but there's no one else in this country who knows what he does. No one.'

I ventured into the practical but excruciating territory of feet, on which he appeared to be hurrying around without the slightest difficulty. 'Look, for months I couldn't take a single step,' he recalled. 'But it got better. It's still there, but it's better. Now, most days I'll just do a basic sandal, with a very simple strap over the foot, but on a day like this, I was meeting a new client, so I thought: Fine, let me do a loafer.' He stretched out something black and suede and most probably Prada. 'Numb!' he exclaimed. 'Totally numb. That's why I'm always bashing them. I'm in the bathroom and the next minute my toe's bleeding. But what am I gonna do? I wrap it up and I *carry on*.'

'But still, you're always running around, always jetting off somewhere. What's the swelling like when you fly?'

He pointed to a table lamp, with a base as wide as a tree trunk, and tossed his hands back into mid-air. 'Like a lamp!'

I tried sharing some anecdotes. I wanted to tell him how similar my experience had been, how I'd also searched for that something, then lost it, and then found it again, but he cut me short: Stephen was not here to listen. He was here to talk. To tell me a story and to bring me a gift of hope. And shallow as he seemed on the surface, I had no inkling of how deep and poignant that message would be.

'Now, listen to me,' he repeated, nudging me again on the knee. 'There's going to come a time when you're going to get better. And you're going to go out and people are going to find you attractive. Now you listen: You sit them right down and you tell them. And if they don't like it, well, that's just their damn problem.'

The phone again. 'Hello? ... Fifteen minutes ... No, I promise.'

'I want to tell you something,' he repeated, speaking slowly. 'Before all this happened, I was an ugly person. Nasty. Rude. Selfish. And do you know what this has taught me ...?' For the first time in the past half hour, there was a deep, carefully considered pause. 'Humility.'

I knew I was looking into the face of a survivor, but it wasn't until then that I sensed a tremor of vulnerability beneath its courageous, expensively moisturised surface. 'I want to leave you with one thing,' he trembled, as he stood up. 'I don't care if you don't remember anything else, but I want you to remember this. There are times when all this will seem like the darkest, darkest time of your life. Times when you can't see anything at all. But if you look, then somewhere, far out in the distance, you'll see the faint lights of a runway. And you take that runway, my boy, and you run with it!'

He bent down and hugged me, and it was only as he stood up that I saw he was smiling through the tears. 'I know there are times when this feels like a punishment,' he shivered. 'Like it's some horrible, horrible curse. But it isn't. I'm telling you, my boy: It's a gift.'

And then he made his way out the front door, sobbing, repeating that same profound declaration of liberation. 'It's a gift. It's a gift. It's a gift.'

* * *

Stephen's words stayed with me for days afterwards. I'd laugh out loud, remembering the rare moments of humour and melodrama he'd brought to this excruciatingly serious experience. 'Like a lamp,' I laughed, looking down at my aching tree trunks. Thank God there were other lamps out there. He had left me feeling just a little bit less alone. And that little bit made all the difference.

It seemed so unfair, really, that Aids was so much a disease of poverty. And that its cruel, unforgiving consequences had so much to do with how much money was available to you. Not everyone had money. And not everyone had parents or friends or medicine or even food. There were some people who had nothing at all. And those people were most probably dead. But hey, what was *fair* about any of this? Not everyone had Aids. Not everyone got a gift.

WORDS

13 January 2005

IN THE COURSE OF my journey, I'd had reason to question many of the words that were being spoken around me, even by me at times. 'Disease' was a pretty accurate term; there had been nothing *easy* about any of this. 'Illness' was troubling, because while my body struggled to recover, spiritually I had probably never been healthier. 'Sickness', meanwhile, was probably better suited to the conspiracy of silence, of which I had been both victim and perpetrator, than to any physical condition.

As Alex had pointed out, there was also something very problematic about the media's persistent use of phrases like 'the battle against Aids', 'the struggle', 'the fight'. What were we fighting: the disease or the people who had been infected with it? Far too often, the answer was the latter.

Another mischievous demon was disguised in the innocuous little question people had poked at me time and time again: 'So, d'you know who gave it to you?' For anyone who had contracted the disease from a supposedly monogamous partner, the answer would have been quite clear, but for me it was far muddier. I was not given the virus; I went out there and helped myself to it.

I am still not certain whether, on the rare occasions of unsafe sex, I simply exposed myself to an immense risk, or whether perhaps, on some subconscious level, I actually sought it out as some kind of twisted, excruciating lesson that I needed to learn. Did I take it? Or did I get it? I don't know. I only know that, in the end, it doesn't matter: For those who survive it, it is, after all, as Stephen had said, a gift.

Ultimately, 'Positive' was probably the most redemptive term in the Aids lexicon, because without an indomitably positive attitude there is undoubtedly little chance of triumphing in the challenges that such a status presents. But 'Aids' is another matter.

I remember how frightened I'd been to say the word in the beginning, how I'd always hidden it behind its safe, polite acronym: HIV. But I forced myself. I said it in shopping malls, around lunch tables, at family gatherings. Aids, Aids, Aids, I said. And the more I said it, the less frightening it seemed, for the more familiar a word becomes, the closer one comes to its meaning, and the easier it becomes to live with.

LAAN

15 January 2005

I HAVE KNOWN ROY SINCE I was fourteen. For more than twenty years, we have been the very best of friends – and the worst, fighting childishly at times and laughing uncontrollably at others. But for all the support and companionship we have shared, over the years our friendship has carried with it a conveyor belt of emotional baggage and has been plagued, all along, with a creepy subtext of competition. 'The Laws of Outshine,' as Roy puts it.

It is rare that we ever address each other by our real names; indeed, one of the more delightful contests had to do with who could think up a more ridiculous name for the other, and scarcely a phone call has been made without this kind of opening surprise: 'Hello, is Eleanor there?' Or Linda, or Beatrice, or Munya or Mrs Awow McGlade. The names have made us shriek with laughter, but, ultimately, we've agreed that one name was the most ridiculous and affectionate of all, and it's stuck. It began as a diminutive of Lauren, if I remember right, but we bastardised it to a point of such delight that it became both our names: Laan and Laan.

Over the past five years, it's come to matter far less which Laan had more in his life and which had less, but occasionally, when we least expected them to, the demons still crept up on us – so much so that at one point in my illness, Laan got grouchy with me. He felt I'd let him down, he said. That we were supposed to be hanging out together, only I had gone out and got Aids, and was stuck in bed. I'd abandoned him, he fumed, and now he had to go out dancing on his own.

On the one hand, I was outraged: What had I abandoned him for? A fucking picnic? Yet, on the other hand, he was quite justified in his experience, and had been brave and honest enough to confront me with it.

But fate is cruel and revelatory. Tragically, just before I got sick, Roy had lost both his parents within the space of a year. So, while he was making his way bravely in the world as an orphan, I was clinging to my life in the tender care of Mom and Dad. On some level, we had both wrestled with the dumb, irrelevant question of who was worse off. Whose story was more painful or frightening? Laan's or Laan's?

Each in our own, excruciating way, had come to realise the value of being alive – for without the weight of death on one side of the scale, it is impossible to truly grasp the weight of life on the other. For Roy, that realisation had come with the terrifying loss of his parents, and for me it had come when I'd got *this* close to losing my own life. And so, fatefully, we had both – separately, but simultaneously – come to grips with the gravity of tragedy, and had finally surrendered to the fact that there was no way of comparing the weight of those tragedies with each other. That loss and pain might be measured in the course of one life, but never against another. That one Laan's fears or joys or success could never weigh any more or less than the other's. That the Laws of Outshine had faded so far into a distant adolescent memory, they had finally ceased to matter.

A week after my birthday, Roy paid me a visit. He'd made a new recording of the CD that had stubbornly refused to play on that blessed pink and orange Sunday of my birthday, and he had it with him. He'd arranged the background music on his Mac, and over it, he had dictated a message to me. He'd been so pissed off that day when the track wouldn't play, and when I finally slipped the disc into the CD player, I understood why: it was one of the most moving gifts I have ever received, spoken straight from the heart, over the gentle tinkling of jazz piano. Laan's voice was direct and tender, and with that conveyor belt cleared of every last, wretched suitcase but love, the message summed up everything that had passed and had miraculously survived between us.

'Hey you,' he began. 'Yes, you! That hysterical-looking girl in the corner. Lorrie-Ann Levin. My dear friend for twenty-seven years – otherwise known as Lauren, Lynne, Belinda, Merle and Clanny-Ann. We've shared a lot together, you and I, from the beginning. We were enemies, and then we became somewhat mysterious lovers. Then we became friends, and then we *still* maintained our friendship. In everything that we have been through – from the scariest, trashiest, skankiest, most hysterical places that we have travelled together, to some very desperate, very sad, but incredibly liberating experiences that I have had with you. This is really a personal Happy Birthday You! Hang in there. Fight the bitch. You are winning. You are a survivor, an inspiration … and a friend. I love you. Happy Birthday, Adam Levin … Mwah!' Soft, sexy beats pulsed out from the speakers, and I wrapped my skinny arms around Laan's big muscled shoulders, as his sweet, heartfelt song of unconditional love rung out forever over the dance beat. 'Mwah … Mwah … Mwah!'

FOURTEEN ROTTEN CHUNKS

31 January 2005

THE NEXT MORNING, MOM and Dad drove me to the dental surgeon. I had prepared meticulously for this auspicious occasion, indulging the dark, ritual humour of my very own Last Supper – a lunch actually; if you must know, a great, mouth-watering slab of medium-rare Portuguese sirloin, topped with a fried egg and doused with dangerous lashings of peri-peri sauce, amid the down-home, vintage splendour of the Radium Beer Hall. With its plastic tablecloths and framed newspaper headlines, the Radium was one of the last remaining joints with an authentic sense of a rapidly disappearing old Johannesburg. And, appropriately, this was the last chunk of steak I would ever chew with my very own, devastatingly decayed molars.

That night I ran through the entire alphabet with my tongue, paying attention to which sounds required the participation of my teeth: The 'c's'; the 's's' and the 'th's', it seemed; the rest could be adequately managed with a tongue, a palate and a couple of lips. It was at moments like these that I'd begun to grasp the gravity of what was soon to happen. But it wasn't until I pulled on a green gown and lay down in yet another clinical white bed that the truly horrifying reality hit home. The HIV. The cancer drugs. The antibiotics. And their pink and white, plastic consequences, smiling eagerly at me from a clear plastic packet.

Indeed, I had been told I would wake up with the

seductively painless and miraculous-sounding solution of 'instant teeth'. The dentures would be placed over my lacerated gums during surgery and would remain there, with the exception of two brief daily antiseptic rinses, for the following week. I was to expect some degree of discomfort, and there would definitely be some swelling, but the dentures would minimise it. 'Keep them out any longer,' I'd been warned, 'and you won't get them back in.'

We had decided to leave the damaged, nicotine-stained front teeth in place for then, in the hope that, with a whole lot of painstaking carpentry, they might still be saved, but with two already gone, the fourteen rotten chunks remaining at the back were beyond hope. And so, I would not be receiving the Hollywood smile I had hoped for; anything new and shiny would be hidden somewhere at the back. Nevertheless, with a terrified child shrieking inconsolably in the bed beside me, I swallowed half a sedative to calm my anxiety and kissed my fourteen rotten chunks goodbye. After all I'd been through, I figured as I drifted into oblivion, this would probably be a piece of cake – which would hopefully be one of the things I could chomp my wounded jaws into, during the next couple of days.

* * *

Anyone who's ever had a general anaesthetic will recall the sense of creepy disorientation that awaits you when you flip open your eyelids. There are moments of crystal lucidity, interspersed with clouds of sheer bewilderment. I asked nervously for a mirror. What I witnessed in its reflection looked something like a large, lopsided onion. The necks of the teeth had been so decayed, I was told, that they'd had to cut most of them out. There was something that resembled a mouth, with a little stream of blood trickling out of the one side, and the entire jaw and neck remained disturbingly anaesthetised. I waited the prescribed hour, by which stage I felt an urgent need to get out of there. To go home and experience something familiar. If there was such a thing.

I propped myself up on the pillows and attempted a cigarette. It was hopeless. I asked for some water to take my anti-retrovirals, but it streamed out of my mouth like a waterfall. My whole head felt numb. Lifeless. Immoveable.

Quen popped in to witness the damage. He didn't say anything about the onion, just mentioned some extremely potent hybrid marijuana he'd just received from California. Despite the temptation, I didn't think it was a very good idea. 'I'll patthh,' I said.

'What? Oh, "pass!" Gotcha.'

A little while later, I asked for some 'thicken thoup'.

'What?'

'Thi-cken th …'

'Sure, I've got some ready,' Mom replied. 'Do you want a mug or a bowl?'

'Mug pleathe,' I attempted. 'But with a thhhpoon.'

Of course I knew that this timeworn Jewish recipe had not only proved a miracle cure for the body, but also for the spirit. But in my case, Chicken Soup for the Soul turned out to be Chicken Soup for the Shirt and the Sheets. Liquid, solid or smoke, I could get nothing into that onion. So I lay there, tired and hungry and terrified that I might never nibble again. I picked up a magazine, but the text seemed to be in a foreign language. I flicked on the TV, but I could barely make sense of the meaningless images on the screen. And each time I laid my dazed, brutalised head on its side, I'd notice a little puddle of blood on the pillow. Its thick, sweet, icky taste clogged stubbornly in my throat. I was frightened to fall asleep, for fear I might choke to death. But I didn't.

By the following morning, I could manage a soft carrot muffin, with dangerously sweet icing. 'The virus likes the sugar,' Stephen had told me, and if my desperate cravings were anything to go by, he was right. But right then I was so utterly relieved to be able to move my jaws, I'd have wolfed down a bath sponge.

As the day progressed, there were moments when I began to feel a little more normal. As the effects of the anaesthetic wore off, I observed, with astonishment, that there was still a world out there, with birds chirping and sunlight dancing radiantly amid the magnificent festival of summer greens, rustling tranquilly through the living room window.

There were moments when I realised I could move my tongue again, only to be ambushed by the weird contours of some bizarre plastic arc lodged in my palate. It felt so utterly alien and invasive, I wondered if I'd ever get used to it. My tongue would need to readjust to the smaller shape of my palate, I'd been told. It amazed me that this miraculous pink organ could teach itself such a thing. And indeed, within a few days, people could actually figure out what I was thaying on the telephone. I prayed for a speedy recovery, because I'd been scheduled to make a thpeech a few days later at a black women's book club.

* * *

As it turned out, the experience was eye-opening and unforgettable. Although the subject was my previous book, *The Wonder Safaris*, my now distant collection of African wanderer's tales, the discussion turned inevitably to the subject of Aids, and to the far more challenging safari I had made over the past year and a half, and all the distance I had travelled while barely stepping foot out of my bedroom.

I felt like Daniel stepping into the lions' den, as I confronted a dozen articulate, professional, young black women, armed with challenging questions for a white boy who had written a book about the black continent. The objections were valid: Why had I written so much about the rest of the continent and so little about my own country? Wasn't it because I had grown up surrounded by comforts that I was so willing to slum it in the continent's grimy, dysfunctional capitals? So I confessed to my own exotic gaze, to the daring adventurous thpirit of a twenty-five-year-old me, and of how enlightening it had been when that journey had finally brought me full thircle, back to the very place I'd thtarted, and kept me there long and immobile enough for me to learn what I'd needed to.

In the course of the afternoon, I experienced tremendous warmth and hospitality, and harboured much resentment at not being able to gnaw my way through the vast, mouth-watering spread of seafood, salads and curries. I also felt greatly privileged to have been granted entry into such an intimate, familial circle. A world that, in post-apartheid South Africa, still remained very much off-bounds to me. One woman spoke of the tragedy of her sister-in-law having recently gone to her grave without the slightest mention of the word 'Aids'. She had left a young daughter, and the family had refused to have her tested, for fear that a positive result would lead to the child being shunned.

I have no doubt there were more stories among those twelve women. They had all undoubtedly known friends and relatives who were sick or had died. Statistically, a couple of them should have been HIV-positive. And yet no more Aids stories came forward. And so, ultimately, the encounter was less a revelation than a confirmation of the immense fog of silence that spread wide and heavy over this disease. Even here, among the most empowered and educated elite of the country's previously disadvantaged population, people seemed ill-equipped to deal with the pandemic that was exploding around them.

* * *

During the week following my surgery, my life had pretty much returned to normal. I was getting a little bored with soup, overcooked pasta and mincemeat, and it was still a distressful struggle each time I wrenched the dentures off my eye teeth and gargled out the muck that had accumulated beneath them. But far quicker than I'd expected, I was beginning to grow used to them.

I'd forgotten, I suppose, just how damn much I'd got used to over the past couple of years. How miraculously my body had adapted itself to such awfully foreign experiences. How it had learnt to tolerate extreme, protracted physical and emotional pain. How astoundingly faithful and resilient it had proved itself to me, in the face of such immense challenges. How it had triumphed in taking the most abnormal circumstances and making them normal.

In the few short days that had passed, I'd been blessed repeatedly with that great warm experience of normality. After any trauma, any violent interruption – be it a scalpel in your mouth, a knife in your gut or a gun to your temple – there is no more exquisitely comforting feeling than that faint glimmer of normality. That profound, astonishing realisation that the sun will probably rise again after the darkest, most terrifying night, and that one's entire, insignificant little world might still be rescued by the two most merciful letters of the English alphabet: O and K.

REN AND TERI

13 February 2005

THE FOLLOWING SUNDAY, REN and Teri invited me over for lunch. The feast was as exquisite as it had been on the past two New Year's Eves. An avocado soup, with notes of ginger and coriander; Ren's macrobiotic buckwheat noodles in rich, dark shoyu sauce, which she'd prepared especially for her newly indentured friend; and a succulent chunk of fillet that Teri had roasted on the fire – the flavour of which was totally wasted on me as I diced it into tiny cubes and washed them down with a glass of water.

After lunch, everyone commented on how different I looked. I gobbled up the compliments. The new, darker shade of hair dye was a definite improvement, but there was something else: if my almost chubby cheeks were anything to go by, Dr S's antibiotics were doing something. My stomach lining had begun regenerating and I was finally absorbing my food. Mom's nightly vegetable soups were no longer just spilling wastefully down a drainpipe. Ren lead me auspiciously to the bathroom, where I leapt excitedly on the scale. It read: 66.2 kilos. A good fifteen more than I'd scaled at my skinniest and pretty much the same as I'd weighed the week before I was diagnosed.

There was good reason to celebrate – as if we'd needed one: a good few bottles of the compulsive grape had already been emptied, and the odd, top-quality reefer had been passed around the table by Byrne, Ren and Teri's die-hard clubber of a tenant. So it figured that our emotions were all a little closer to the surface than usual.

I looked at Teri, sitting across from me, and then turned to Byrne. It seemed fitting to pay tribute to two beautiful friends who had shown me so much love in the course of my illness. Scarcely a day had passed without a phone call or a visit, at the end of which they would both hug me so hard I'd fear my skinny ribs would crack. 'You know something amazing?' I said to Byrne. 'When I was first diagnosed, there were lots of people who just walked away and disappeared. I'm sure you know them all from the club scene, but I haven't laid eyes on them since. Gone. But Ren and Teri did exactly the opposite. We didn't know each other very well before I got sick, but the moment it happened, they just came closer and closer to me, and they've stayed right here at my side, through every messy, frightening moment of it.'

'I know,' Byrne smiled.

* * *

There is something very moving about Teri's hazel eyes, especially when they crinkle up and get all watery, and I looked right into them as she responded, softly and thoughtfully, as always. 'Ad,' she stammered. 'I don't know if you realise what this has been for all of us. Just being here, being so close to you, through all of this. It's been the most amazing *gift*. It's brought out so many things we would never have come across if it hadn't been for this experience.'

I reached for her hand, deeply humbled. Who would ever have imagined something so ghastly could carry with it anything so magical? Life never failed to surprise you, did it?

And for the first time, it dawned on me what sheer positivity my disease had serendipitously brought about in the lives of so many others, and that had I tested negative in the beginning, we might all have missed out on so much. 'It's crazy,' I said. 'But I guess the worst experiences bring out the very best in us. The most courage, the most love, the most intensive care.'

Outside, the sun had already dipped into the horizon,

and the six remaining lunch guests stepped onto the stoep and looked out into the pale orange Jo'burg sky, and over Ren and Teri's gracefully terraced garden. The leaves were twinkling grey and mauve in the dusk light, and we sat ourselves in a circle. Then, one by one, three of us each braved a little song to capture the afternoon in melody, accompanied only by the chirping of cicadas. Someone crooned a little Cole Porter. Then Zingi closed his eyes and channelled Björk with such perfectly frozen timing he transported us all to Iceland. Applause!

I knew what I wanted to sing. It was a Swahili love song I had first heard in a dark room in Zanzibar, from the voice of Bi Kidude, a legendary ninety-year-old Taarab singer, and then learnt, word by word, from an Omani street hustler, as we swung together in a hammock on the edge of the Indian Ocean. I had long forgotten the song's translation, but somehow every last syllable had stayed with me, and I sang it as he had taught it to me, pausing long and slow and rolling my eyes back on each lilting semi-tone. Applause!

Encore, they said. I thought briefly until I stumbled across a few verses of U2 that I've always loved, and I changed just a few of the words, as I belted them forth from the bottom of my gut, holding the notes as long and clear as my tar-drenched lungs could manage:

I have climbed / Highest mountains
I have swum / Deepest seas
On my Won-der Sa-far-I / I liked to wander
But I still / Hadn't found / What I's looking for

Looking for / Looking fo-o-or
I still / Hadn't found / What I's looking for.

So I climbed / In my bed-sheets
Nearly laid / Down and died
On my Aids-sa-far-I! / And I came to wonder
If I just / Hadn't found / What I's looking for
Looking for / Looking fo-o-or
If I just / Hadn't found / What I's looking for.

A LITTLE COURAGE

18 February 2005

IT WAS FRIDAY NIGHT. Like so many lately, the past few days had been so drenched in richness I'd worried at times that my little brain might explode in its endeavour to absorb and make sense of it all. My good friend James had come to visit me from New York and I had been staying at my house for the past week. The hours had been so blissfully complete with work and people that it was not until around 8 p.m. that evening that I found myself, as we all do at moments: alone and a little frightened. I listened for the comforting sounds of Mom tinkering in the kitchen, or the distant blaring of the TV in the study, with Dad dozing in front it, but I heard nothing: only the quintessential silence of solitude.

Through it all, I had come to realise that this would ultimately prove the true test of my recovery, the reckoning of any real transformation: just how toughly I had steeled myself to endure the periods of loneliness that might lie ahead. It was a question that lies buried somewhere in all of us: If and when it came to the crunch, could I do it solo?

There had been times when I'd run as far and fast as I could from that feeling – when I had driven myself drunk into dangerous territories of lies, so acute was my condition of fright. But I no longer had the luxury of such options. Scarcely able to stand, let alone walk or drive at night, I could not begin to entertain the sort of dark inappropriate solutions I had previously explored. I had lost myself and my body in the game of prevention, and now, in turn, its very fragility prevented *me* from using its sexual charms to magic up instant intimacies. For two years, for its very survival, it had numbed itself into celibacy and erased all desire from its psyche. I had masturbated three times during that period – but only to check (Success!). Two years? It seemed like a lifetime ago. But it wasn't: it was only a lifestyle ago.

Some other night, I'd have probably just slipped into a TV coma, or numbed myself out on a joint, but on that particular night, the solitude was too haunting for any such cowardly refuge. I listened through the great, hollow echo and thought my way through the maze of loneliness. Could the rich memories of the past few days suffice to ease the evening's lonely ache? I wondered. Or might the thought of faraway lovely ones bring some warmth to chilling oneness? Hmmn. It was worth a bash.

I wrote to Marcos in Brazil, to Tess in Italy, to Hein in Thailand. And for those couple of hours, I enjoyed the rich pleasure of their company, but afterwards, I had still not quelled the rustle of restlessness beneath – so it was around 10 p.m., I guess, that a quite terrifying idea slipped into my mind. What if I went *out*? What if I just leapt into a cab and hopped off to a bar like I'd done a million times a million years ago? What if ...

I sobered myself with the absurdity of the proposition. I'd attempted venturing *out* after sunset a few weeks back and it had been a disaster. It was my friend Verna's farewell party. Despite the safety of friends and the great efforts Vern had made to accommodate me on a cushioned pool lounger, my attempt had endured little more than an hour. The awkwardness of being horizontal while everyone else chatted vertically, and the challenge of disguising my pain in the light-hearted party atmosphere, had left me far more alienated than had I stayed at home. I felt conquered afterwards. Deeply disappointed in myself and the universe.

With the benefit of such experience, I had good reason to believe that the mischievous little plot that had crept into my mind was doomed to pathos. I pictured myself: hobbling into a club after two years of absence, tumbling down a flight of stairs before a gaggle of cackling queens, or hiding behind a pillar, ostracised by the unattainable superficialities of the scene. Exposed, or worse: invisible again? How long would I manage on my feet? Where would I sit? Would anyone come over and talk to me?

Hmmn. I tried my luck for an escort but only came up with regretful apologies or voicemail: fatefully, if this was to prove a true test of independence, the evening would offer no easy solutions. And so I paced the house in my slippers, testing my mobility and endurance. I felt riddled with uncertainty, and yet, beneath it, I was charged with an urgent and inexorable bravado to escape the prison of my fears and make some sort of crazed, dubious attempt, no matter how humiliating the consequences, and before I knew it, I found myself standing in front of the mirror, contemplating a long, matchstick-concealing sleeve and figuring out the possibilities of my hair. This was going to require a little courage.

I hesitated before dialling for a taxi, but my fingers did it for me. 'Five minutes? … Okay.' And there was no turning back: If I didn't try, I'd never know.

* * *

As the fate of the yellow street lights would have it, I recognised the driver's toothy grin immediately. He'd chauffeured me a few weeks previously, and the three hippopotamine chunks jutting out from his upper jaw had precipitated an instant stream of disclosure on my part. 'Remember me?' I beamed. 'Look, I got the new teeth.'

'So quickly?' he replied, glancing across.

'Yeah, it really wasn't that bad in the end.'

'But costly,' he lamented. 'So, where are you going?'

'Melville,' I declared. 'The corner of Fourth and Main.'

'Why are you going out on your own?' he fussed. 'Mustn't I take you to your mother's house again?'

'No,' I replied, rehearsing some requisite nonchalance. 'I just felt like going out tonight.'

'Well, just don't drink too much,' he tut-tutted.

'One or two,' I winked, as I limped up to the entrance.

* * *

I have known the doorman forever and he recognised me immediately. 'Shabbat Shalom!' he announced. 'Do you know I nearly died? I had a *stroke* two years ago!' I took a brief stab at empathy. 'Actually, me too …' I attempted, but he didn't hear me, for he was already perfunctorily saying, 'Good to see you, my boy. Go in and have a good time.'

I bought a beer and found myself a safe perch on the balcony. I caught the odd glint of recognition but no one spoke to me, and so, while the bar filled up, I sat silently on my own, stoically resisting the urge to flinch each time someone stepped on my feet, sipping my beer and doing my best not to look needy.

Those first couple of hours were dismal. The moment I set foot in that environment, I was overcome with the same damn insecurities that put me in this predicament in the first place, only all the more intensely: Was I cute enough? Was anyone cruising me? How much of a freak did I look like? Could anyone see how lost I felt?

Evidently someone could. 'Adam!' I heard from a distance. It was the same guy who had left me feeling so invisible in the mall a few weeks back, and he was making his way towards me, looking quite the picture of wholesomeness. 'I'm so sorry,' he said. 'I've thought about you so many times since then. I mean, for obvious reasons, I really didn't recognise you at first, but afterwards I felt so awful about it … But anyway, how are you doing? You're looking so much better.'

I took his number and promised to call. I was delighted

to hear the triumphant thump of dance music again, and to sit observing this strangely familiar world, of sleeveless T-shirts, tans and biceps. But now I wanted to be invisible, to sip my beer without the brief, awkward glances I couldn't help but notice. I wanted to watch, but the thought of *being* watched seemed unbearable. I wanted no pity or scrutiny: I wanted to flee, but the prospect of the doorman enquiring, 'Leaving already?' kept me on my perch, sipping bravely, until finally some guy came over and struck up a conversation. 'I like your shirt …'

He was attractive, though a bit too polished for my taste, but I was astonished that someone was actually offering to buy me a drink. Lying emaciated in a hospital bed, the possibility of anyone ever desiring me again had seemed utterly absurd, and yet, after fifteen minutes of chit-chat, it became quite clear that this man was making advances; rubbing his leg against me; telling me about the poppers he liked to snort while having sex.

Suddenly, I was haunted by a sentence from Stephen's Gift: 'You sit them right down, my boy, and you tell them, and if they don't like it, it's their damn problem.' But I didn't. I was flattered, frightened, even tempted at moments, and then, from somewhere deep inside, the clear voice of reason rang out to my rescue: Baby, we haven't had sex for two years. Now we're gonna go and throw that away with someone we're not even wild about, who probably won't remember us tomorrow? We don't think so.

I pulled away and plucked up the nerve to hobble back to the bar and make the promised attempt at mingling. 'No matter how humiliating the consequences.' Right? With a couple of lagers in me, my mood had shifted. I felt stronger. Cheekier. Brave enough to toss the odd, vaguely suggestive innuendo at whoever happened to be standing nearby. But the catalyst was an insane black queen, who spotted me across the room and yelled, 'Aren't you supposed to be dead?'

And, as she made her way towards me, I was certain I was in for a night of brave honesties. 'I need to ask you something,' she proceeded theatrically, her arm draped across the shoulders of a cute young blond. 'Would you be interested in doing a line of coke off this man's chest?'

'Well, thanks, but no thanks,' I replied. 'But I'll come with for moral support if you like.' Clearly this held little appeal, and they scuttled off towards the bathroom. I looked around, feeling strangely lost, until I spotted someone I knew sitting nearby. I knew he was a brother with Aids but that he never spoke about it, so I invited him to join me for a joint on the balcony. 'I certainly hope you aren't policemen,' I barked at the two buffed boys seated at a nearby table. 'Not if you'll give us a puff,' one of them volleyed. So we lit up.

As we chatted, I was aware of a volume knob turning inside me. There were two young queens seated down the way, and the more feminine of the two ventured a touchingly clichéd question. 'Excuse me, can I ask you all something? We're having a debate here: Are you born gay or is it something that happens while you're growing up?' A chorus of confused voices rallied hurriedly in response, until finally I stomped down my beer. 'I've figured it out,

Miss Thing,' I declared. 'You were born gay; but he wasn't. Now go figure!'

My feet were screaming in pain, but the voice inside was screaming louder. The more cowardly the conversation proceeded without mention of the word Aids, the more determined I became to shatter the ghostly silence thumping somewhere beneath the deafening speakers and shout its name at the top of my voice: Aids! I no longer wanted to be invisible; I wanted to be right there: loud, fearless and in any face that dared look into mine.

I had hoped that my noisiness might elicit some disclosure from my friend, but it didn't. He remained conspicuously silent and departed with polite promises of a lunch date. 'He seemed real edgy when you brought up that subject,' one of the buff boys remarked. 'Yes, of course he is,' I replied. ''Cos he's trapped in his own fucking silence!' Then suddenly, without any warning, this virtual stranger leapt up and held out his big brawny arms. 'I've got to hug you,' he insisted. I obliged. It was sincere, though quite impersonal, and yet I'd already begun to observe what potent emotive responses my bravado was bringing out in the sea of mediocrity that surrounded me.

I limped back for another drink. There was a tanned, well-built, good-looking man standing next to me. He gave me a cursory glance – out of pity, I guessed. So I ordered my damn beer. And then I noticed that he was looking again, but this time with a wary curiosity. 'Can I help you?' I smirked.

'Well, maybe,' he pouted drunkenly.

I spotted the coke queen, back from the loo, but with

a new friend. 'It's like, wow!' she shrieked, gesturing at me. 'She's white. She's dying and next thing I hear she's launching a book in Hyde Park!'

Everyone heard. And everyone knew. But the thunderous public utterance of the word 'dying' no longer scared me: in fact, it left me feeling even braver. 'I need to ask you something,' she persisted, like a scratched vinyl. 'Would you be interested in doing a line of coke off this man's dick?'

She didn't wait for an answer, for I had already turned away and realised that the enigmatic stranger at my side had fixed his gaze candidly upon mine. 'D'you know what?' he said openly. 'I look out there and I see nothing. But when I look at you, I see something ... I don't know what it is, but I think I like it.'

'Yes, of course you do,' I replied smugly, realising, to my amazement, that his curious gaze had shifted into something far more unlikely: desire. 'I like you,' he said softly. I liked him too. I liked the way his every utterance was so totally unpredictable. And I sensed that beneath the wholesome exterior, there was something quite extraordinary about him: if he was so acutely attuned to courage, he must have known deep pain at some stage. He'd made a brave declaration, and although I had no doubts as to its utter sincerity in that instant, I was dubious whether the sentiment could endure the brave, intoxicated mess of the moment. 'I don't care!' he boomed unexpectedly. 'Come! I'll fuck you. You'll fuck me. Whatever!'

'Why?' I countered. There had been people who'd made desperate attempts to contact me when they heard I was ill, after twenty years of silence, and there were also freaks out there who wanted to have sex with someone with Aids – perhaps to shatter their own denial, perhaps out of some insane recklessness or misguided masochism. Who knew? I was pretty certain his intentions were more sincere than that. And yet, despite the exhilarating shiver of serendipity tingling through me, I knew I could no longer sate myself on transient sentiment: not after everything I'd been through. 'So give me your phone number,' I demanded, reaching for my cellphone.

'No!' he snapped, and walked away.

Presently, out of nowhere, another unknown face appeared. It was that of a busty, blonde babe who'd been eavesdropping – like who hadn't? And it was only moments before she too had her arms wrapped tightly around me. Her brother had survived Aids, she revealed, and she wanted to be close to me, to display her tribute and encouragement for the little courage that had driven me out that evening. 'It's wonderful, isn't it?' I grinned. 'Nightclubs are so full of surprises.'

* * *

In the hours that followed, things only got louder and braver and messier. 'Do you want to do a line of coke off this man's …?'

'No!' I despaired. But hey, I washed down the lagers regardless. What with my plastic teeth, every second sentence was demanding tedious repetition, but every now and then I'd turn and behold those same lost, beautiful eyes transfixed on mine. All night, he'd persisted thus: scouring the room like a predator, and circling steadily back to my gaze. 'You know what?' he confessed. 'When I first saw you, I thought you were retarded.'

'And now …' I smiled gently. 'Do you still think I'm retarded?'

He looked at me very warmly. 'Fuck, I don't want any of this,' he shrugged, looking out at the remaining clutches of handsome strangers, yakking on about distressed jeans or star signs. 'I don't think you realise this,' he urged. 'But I don't come here all the time. I come here once in a blue moon. And for once, I think I'm feeling something.'

He hugged me tight. I so wanted to believe him – to dream again that a moment might last forever, but I couldn't – not any more. 'So give me your damn number!' I challenged, but he only turned and walked away again. He couldn't believe himself, I guess.

I glanced at my phone. How the hell could it already read 5:07? I hadn't planned on lasting an hour, and now, so quickly, the bar was already dripping empty, and as the last stragglers swayed stubbornly on to a fabulously ironic remix of 'Hopelessly Devoted', I stepped out onto the balcony and called for a taxi.

A few moments later, I brushed past the doorman and out into the scary, drunken morning light. As I climbed into the cab, I saw handsome staggering back and forth on the pavement, fumbling with his cellphone – looking for God's number, I presume.

'I hope we meet again sometime,' I called out, in honour of the moments of sincere possibility that had slipped like grains of precious, pink sand through our fingers, but he was evidently too wasted to hear me. It didn't matter. The evening had been so rich with revelations. Who cared if I wasn't going home with someone? I was leaving with something: Integrity.

I felt damn proud of my feet, and prouder still of myself. All those dark, frightening months I'd been trapped in my bed-sheets: this place hadn't changed a bit. The same beautiful men. The same brawny biceps, eyeing one another across the room. The same crotches, hardening in lusty advances. The same bullshit. But *I* had changed. Somehow, in the course of this crazy, bewildering safari, I had changed a great deal.

* * *

As the car crept through the pale, slumbering landscape of the suburbs, I realised something quite astonishing: while my fragile physicality had still terrified and repulsed the superficial hunks in my midst, my sheer courage had fiercely attracted others towards me. Wow! What a difference that might make in the long run. What brave souls might I yet encounter on a path that was so much richer and more meaningful – instead of the shallow assholes I'd wasted so much of myself on in the past?

That instant of realisation filled me with tremendous hope and excitement. All those warm, close embraces of affirmation from complete strangers. All that gorgeous honesty. And nothing sacrificed to expedience.

By the time the car pulled to a halt, the sky was already pinkening with the optimism of a brand new dawn. It had been a fucking beautiful night, and with some anonymous taxi driver looking on, I hobbled, trashed, along the last steps to my front gate. And hey, I felt fucking beautiful too.

MIRACLES
20 February 2005

WHILE I WAS RAISED in the proud tradition of Judaism, when it came to personal belief systems, my father went to great lengths to instil a committed sense of atheism in his son – and for the most part, I thank him for it. I have always prided myself on this sensible, logical take on the universe and, for most of my life, have remained staunchly dismissive on matters with even the slightest smack of hocus pocus. It appears, however, that two events in my life were destined to bring about a small but significant shift in my consciousness.

The first – the decade I spent wandering through Africa – I had summed up in *The Wonder Safaris*. I had journeyed long and hard to place myself in the proximity of people who still lived out ancient traditions, and lacked access to information and technology, and the experience had filled me with all the wonder I'd hoped for. I can't say I believed in God at the end of it, but I certainly felt *wonder-full*.

My subsequent two-year journey with Aids, however, was to prove a far greater challenge to my proud tradition of rationality. There were indeed a couple of moments on this *Aidsafari* when I found myself praying and pleading for mercy, and, hard as it was to admit, I was *praying* to someone or something greater than myself – to God, if you like. Thus far, my prayers had been answered, and the blessing of my resurrection had demanded a certain transformation: I had no choice but to feel *mercy-full*.

Given that there had been a God when it suited me, to denounce that belief once the urgent moments of mortality had passed would have been an act of gross fickleness and hypocrisy. When it came to the crunch, I had reluctantly, in sheer desperation, turned to *believing*, and in that act, I had committed myself as a believer.

In the humbling course of my journeys – both inside and out – I had come to develop a healthy respect for miracles: I was, after all, their living proof. And although I still think their occurrence is due partly to the potency of a collective subconscious, I can no longer glibly dismiss the role of some supreme being in their making. Either way, I am certain that developing a deep faith in such wondrous affairs will, in turn, make for a life that is rich with surprises and inexplicable coincidences. If I am willing to open my eyes to their possibility, miracles will continue to surface magically everywhere around me. Believe and they will come.

AIDSURVIVAS

27 February 2005

A WEEK LATER, I FLEW down to Cape Town to spend some time with my sisters and some of my dearest mates. The trip was revelatory in that I discovered, by grinning and bearing my pain, just how much of what I had previously thought impossible was quite manageable.

During those couple of weeks, I found myself: dancing all night on those *feet*, fending for myself, and getting quite deliciously laid by someone brave and exciting enough to be with me. I also attended days of mind-exploding discussions at the Design Indaba and covered a beer-tottering tour of the gay shebeens in the city's townships for a magazine article. Not bad for a damaged, differently abled survivor of a clutch of life-threatening diseases.

The following weekend I hooked up with a long-lost friend, Arend, affectionately known as Rind. Rind had been just as sick as I had, and was recovering bravely at the time. We had communicated by cellphone over the past two years – occasionally comparing cell counts or bitching about our medication – and remote as they might have been, those odd connections had provided me with rare moments of solace during my darkest days.

We had both partied so wildly in the past. Rind's brilliant, absurd humour and unpredictable nerve had always made for an explosive energy whenever we happened to hook up. Now, fatefully, we had made our separate journeys to hell – but we were both back, and I was quite certain that the moment we'd set for our reunion, at a café on Cape Town's Greenmarket Square, held within it the promise of sheer pandemonium.

Within five minutes, it was clear that I was not to be disappointed: a few hilarious one-liners and a cup of filter coffee down the line, and we were already publicly swapping T-shirts and transforming the pavement into an impromptu catwalk extravaganza to the thumping of a conveniently placed band of African drummers. As for props: the Hindu prayer shawl I happened to have in my bag proved most useful in the spontaneous whirling dervish spectacle that ensued. It was great to see Rind again. We had always been unstoppable together in public, and after all we had survived, we were triple trouble. If my faith in miracles required any reinforcement, our reunion that Saturday was to do the trick.

Despite the fact that we are both gay and often outrageously proud of that fact, it was indeed sheer coincidence that it happened to be Cape Town's Gay Pride Parade that morning. We had both attended Pride many times. We'd been there and done it and were far more interested in our own private parade than in taking part in any grandscale affair, full of amateur party animals who could only pull together a look for one day each year. However, as fate would have it, we decided to make a short, precarious ride up the road on Rind's gleaming new red motorbike. I clutched my friend around his waist and felt a light breeze through my hair. It was chance alone that crossed our path with that of the Pride parade, as it proceeded along its route.

'Should we do it?' Rind yelled. 'But of course!' I yelled back. He flung a sharp left that very nearly hurled us onto the pavement. We sneaked into the passing retinue of floats, Rind's hand pressing firmly on the hooter. I yanked the prayer shawl from my backpack, and held it high and proud as we sped along, tooting and yelling triumphantly, 'Watch out! We've got Aids!' and 'Viva! Aidsurvivas!' – and for anyone who might have thought this was a gratuitous or distasteful display of irony, it wasn't: it was true.

That brief, unforgettable journey held great resonance for me. It captured all the camp grandeur of the scene in *Priscilla, Queen of the Desert*, when the bus makes its way through the Australian Outback, with that giant silver shoe atop it, and that magnificent trail of silver cloth fluttering in the breeze. There was also an unmistakable echo of Che Guevara and his companion, making their journey through South America, as recreated in Walter Salles' spectacular film, *The Motorcycle Diaries*. The outrageous spectacle we created was all that and more, rolled into one – a tribute to our mutual, unlikely experience of survival and a celebration of the courageous liberation that had blossomed from it.

How could I experience such a marvellously serendipitous triumph without believing in miracles? That we had *made it*, that the parade had found us, and that, disabled as we both were, we'd somehow managed to toot and screech our way along its entire course must surely have been the work of something far greater than ourselves. A miracle? Indeed. I had come to believe in them, and they were coming, fast and furious.

Nevertheless, it soon became clear that there were some among us who were less than delighted by our shameless exhibitionism. Indeed, when the parade reached its destination, and we continued to prance and shout the unspeakable name of Aids at the after-party, I slumped, exhausted, into a vacant seat, only to elicit a rather unambiguous response from the evidently bitter queen seated next to me. 'Fuck off,' he barked.

'Oh, I'm sorry, my feet are sore … I just needed to sit down for a moment.'

'*Get lost!*' he spat, in no uncertain terms.

I felt a little wounded, and retreated quietly into the shade for a few minutes. But it was only afterwards, on reflection, that I realised just why our loud and proud ownership of the virus within us had elicited such aggression. The unhappy gay lad in question was probably dealing with some degree of denial at that moment, I suspected. Perhaps he had recently tested positive. Perhaps, like me, he had found himself in the throes of unsafe sex at moments, and had been too frightened to get tested. Perhaps, like so many others in the eye of the Aids tornado, he was too terrified to acknowledge its existence.

If any of my suspicions were correct, then surely the last thing the poor frightened wretch needed at that moment was a couple of unstoppable fags screeching 'Aidsurvivas' at the top of their voices. But that was his business: Rind and I had more serious business to attend to – dancing – and I left it to sweet Quen, who, on hearing the news, took it upon himself to sidle up to *the angry one* a little while later and whisper politely, 'If you can't be nice ... then go home!'

I ran into a few people who expressed some concern about me getting plastered in the sunshine. This situation was easily remedied. Always ready for a new look, I snapped a couple of leafy branches from a nearby tree and shoved them into my sunglasses, creating something of an indigenous Carmen Miranda moment. I looked for Rind, who had hurried off on a mission to take his medication on stage, and when I finally found him, I pleaded, 'Don't *leave* me this way.' He didn't. Indeed, it was only many hours later that he finally sped me home. I held my tired arms around his waist and clenched my stiff, sore feet to the bike's footrests. As a big orange *ilanga* dipped into the silvery Atlantic horizon, I felt the wind of miracles shooting triumphantly through my hair. And as Priscilla, Che and a cast of proud, exhausted Aidsurvivas sped away into the sunset, a vague thought crossed my mind: Hmmn. Rather a lot of passengers for a small red bike.

WHO'D HAVE THOUGHT?
29 February 2005

A COUPLE OF DAYS LATER, I got the chance to finally sit down with a cuppa and chat with Kate about the memoir I'd been scribbling. She had recently made me the central character of her second novel, *Spite*, and had dedicated the book to me. She was thus rather put out that she did not feature extensively in this text, and spitefully proposed not to read a word of it on its publication.

'You are in the text, goddammit!' I beseeched her. 'But the book is all about everyone who was physically present, and for of a lot of the time, you weren't around, Kate. Of course you were always with me. If it wasn't for you and Alex ambushing me with your concern at that dreadful dinner – if it wasn't for you seeking out Dr D behind my back, in an act of pure, desperate love, mate – let's face it, I probably wouldn't be here.'

'Hmmn,' Kate mused, almost convinced.

We spoke about my recent discoveries – about how I had realised what a gift this horrific experience had turned out to be, for me and for all those around me. About how much I would have missed out on had I tested negative in the first place. And indeed, in my coming to terms with the whole *fuckin' hectic* saga, I'd almost convinced myself that this had been some fateful lesson I'd needed to learn. That I was somehow better off for everything I'd been through. If only to wreak a sliver of meaning from the experience, I suppose, I'd needed to find some purpose in all the pain and terror.

Kate shook her head gravely. She's such a damn smartass, I was certain I was due for some snappy, ironic retort, but on reflection I have never seen my dear mate look quite so serious. 'No, Ad,' she said. 'I so so wish that none of this had ever happened. It really wasn't necessary. I so wish you'd have got to this point in some other way, without all that ghastly suffering.'

Excruciating as it was, I had no choice but to admit that Kate's words held some wisdom. Perhaps none of it had been necessary. 'You might be right, mate,' I conceded. 'Maybe I could've. Maybe I could've rescued myself from some rapidly approaching spiritual death by taking some other, less frightening path. Maybe I could have saved my life without the *aid* of Aids. Maybe not ... Anyhow, mate, I guess we'll never know.'

An eerie silence hovered for a few moments and then Kate brightened. 'I'll tell you something,' she smirked. '*Who'd have thought, mate?* All those years – such a whinger, such a complainer, such a fusspot about the tiniest little thing – and then when it comes to the crunch, hallelujah! He's a swimmer! Really,' she shrugged, rolling her eyes in amazement. 'Who'd ever have thought?'

LIVING WITH IT

17 March 2005

AROUND 3 P.M. ON THURSDAY afternoon, I had my first appointment in over two months with Dr S. I felt proud not to have bothered him with my daily trials, and to have taken on a greater personal responsibility for my well-being. There was reason to celebrate: since I had last stepped on his scale, I had gained ten kilos. Thanks to his ingenious diagnosis and treatment of the tuberculosis in my stomach (the incidence of which I had later learnt was extremely rare), I had been able to absorb my food and medicines. As a result, my body no longer looked nor functioned like a drainpipe, and every day I was bumping into folks who expressed their relief and delight at how much better I was looking. Granted, to most of them, it must have seemed as though I had made an amazing turnaround, and was now cheerily on the road to a full recovery. But things are not always what they seem.

Indeed, the results of my blood tests proved disappointing. My all-telling CD4 count had climbed a miserable 4 points since my last spell in hospital, leaving it at a still perilous 93. And while I had learnt that it was my body, and not only my cell count, that was to prove my bible, the tedious crawl back to health was requiring immense faith and perseverance. Although I had been doing much more, going out at night when the occasion required it, and actually *living* to some degree, this was due more to a steely determination on my part than any substantial relief from discomfort. Yes, pain, my faithful companion, was still constantly in the picture.

I had been to see a pain therapist at one point, and her wisdom had proved extremely helpful to me. She was a qualified Polish anaesthesiologist, and evidently very passionate about her vocation. She also struck me as somewhat eccentric, as she sat me down to what was intended to be a three-hour introductory session on the subject: Ouch! I managed to hustle her down to two.

'So let us begin,' she instructed, leading up to a deceptively simple question. 'What is pain?' According to the World Health Organisation, she reported, there is a very simple, universal definition at our disposal. 'Pain is a physical and emotional sensory experience of discomfort, associated with tissue damage, actual or potential.' It sounded quite familiar, yet while adequate as a physiological explanation, it still did not address the psychological experience for me.

Pain is abstract and mysterious. I guess the most difficult issue for me is the utter subjectivity of the matter. How can I ever hope to communicate my experience to anyone who isn't living inside my body? How many expletives might I blare with any hope of expressing the severity of my discomfort? And how can I be certain that what seems so unbearable to me is any more distressing than, say, your grumbling old aunt's back complaint? Well, I can't.

Furthermore, while there have been times when my pain has reduced me to a helpless, whimpering wreck on my bed, there have been other times when I've managed, inexplicably, to dance all night on those same aching feet. There have been times when I had feared that its severity was beyond my capability, only to have it intensify. The only explanation Dr S had been able to provide was that the body had its own mysterious mechanisms for coping with pain. 'Mysterious' didn't help demystify much, but the pain therapist did. The key issue, she explained, was control. 'Either you control the pain,' she stated categorically. 'Or the pain controls you.'

Next, she provided me with some disturbingly realistic statistics on the subject. Acute pain is defined as a condition that lasts shorter than three months and generally does not recur. Chronic pain is another matter. Chronic pain can last as long as the rest of one's life. It was no mystery what category I fell into. Statistically, she reported, 60 per cent of chronic pain conditions are not curable. Encouragingly, however, with professional intervention, the same percentage of sufferers will learn to manage their condition and rehabilitate themselves to live relatively normal lives. Hope!

Scientifically, the study of pain is a relatively new discipline. Indeed, we know very little about this disturbing sensation, and it is only recently that pain has been recognised, not as a symptom of other conditions, but as a disease in its own right. Happily, this has resulted in some progressive and encouraging new approaches to treatment.

Although a multidisciplinary approach was developed in the fifties, it has taken decades for its implementation to kick in. Essentially, it comprises three critical elements: pharmacological, non-pharmacological and psychological. Pharmacologically, I am already swallowing as much as I could possibly hope to. I have run the gamut of prescription analgesics. I am now in recovery from morphine addiction and am coping with less effective but safer painkillers, with their own set of side effects.

The non-pharmacological aspect entails a range of treatments such as physiotherapy and acupuncture. None of these have proved very useful for me, but the basic premise that exercise stimulates the production or endorphins – the body's natural painkillers – has proved most effective. The more active I am, and the less I sit, paralysed, thinking about nothing but pain, the less it controls my life. It is the third aspect, however, that interests me the most. Living with constant pain had been a huge psychological challenge for me, and over the past few months I have made substantial progress.

While I can't say that that my physical effects have diminished much, more and more I've grasped what it means to become the Chief Executive Officer of my body. Most of the time, I refuse to let my excruciating employees at the far end of my legs dictate my day. I have accomplished many things in spite of their constant irritation, and that has empowered me. Generally, people I meet have no clue as to my enduring 'sensory experience of discomfort', but, as I have learnt, the less I speak about pain or focus on it, the better I feel. Distraction has proved a very good medicine.

There are also times when it helps me to think of my discomfort as something with a greater purpose: to perceive it as a constant physical reminder of the suffering of so many others – as a metaphor for all that is not right on this planet. For indeed, if there is any possible reason for this terrifying pandemic at this stage of human evolution,

I figure, it might be this: to engender within us all a greater sense of compassion for the pain of others.

And so, with each step I take on these obnoxious feet, I am compelled into a state of empathy for a world encumbered with cruel stigmas, ghastly imbalances of wealth, and dubious access to treatment, medication and survival. Yes, I have been spared the utter destitution of poverty that so often surrounds Aids, but I have not been spared its pain, and whatever the specialists tell me, I am not certain that I will ever again experience a moment of total liberation from it.

So yes – it hurts. But the less I dwell on that, the less it hurts. Aids hurts. Even *life* hurts sometimes. Is there any justice in that? I doubt it. But justice has nothing to do with Aids or pain or life. I think I should pin a little note on my forehead, just in case I am tempted to forget something absolutely critical to my physical and emotional well-being. 'Remember: Nothing is *fair* about Aids.'

* * *

Dr S made some small alterations to my medication in the hope that these would help boost my immunity. He then proceeded to examine me. There were some new Kaposi's lesions on my foot, but instead of full-scale chemotherapy, he hoped that locally injected doses of the right drug would do the trick this time. 'Are you ready?' he asked, the needle poised in his fingers. 'Sure,' I replied. 'You know I might sing though.'

It is a very sensitive part of the body, the inner arch of the foot, even without nerve damage – and indeed, as Dr S drove the needle into the taut layer of skin, I found myself not singing, but screaming. As often, however, the good doctor managed to distract me from my brief surge of agony with a casual anecdote. He spoke, surprisingly, of how, despite completing his medical studies, he had never planned to make his life as a doctor, but had hoped rather to become a Latin teacher.

Nevertheless, some time around 1982, fate had found him working as an ordinary GP, and he was still wondering which direction to take when the local medical community encountered its first case of a still unknown disease. For lack of understanding, the perplexing condition was referred to as GRID (Gay Related Immune Deficiency syndrome) at the time, and Dr S was uncomfortable with the stigmas implicit in this diagnosis. In general, he recalled, the medical community concurred that this was some 'obscure, insignificant condition' and left the case to a specialist to 'go and sit in a corner and fiddle with'.

It is hard to believe that this happened a little more than twenty years ago – that, in two short decades, this 'obscure, insignificant condition' would erupt into the greatest crisis facing the future of humanity.

Fatefully, during that time, Dr S gave up his dreams of teaching Latin and forged on with 'the silly business of medicine'. The only area that had ever been of vague interest to him was the study of infectious diseases, and it was thus that he chose to spend the following five years earning his professorship in virology. Of course, he had no idea at the time that the treatment of the 'obscure, insignificant condition' he'd encountered would ultimately become his vocation, and that he would emerge as one of this country's most respected experts in the field. I'm sure he had no inkling of how many lives he would come to save in the process – or indeed that mine would have been one of them.

* * *

It would have been so tidy and convenient if I could have used this visit to Dr S as a final punctuation to this memoir. If only he could have offered me a clean bill of health, I could have concluded this tale with a happy ending. But life is neither tidy nor convenient. And, happy as it might have been, it would, nevertheless, have been an ending, and as of this moment, I am most pleased to report that this tale has not yet met its finality. Indeed, for those who survive, living with Aids makes each day a brave new beginning – a day of fear, suffering, inconveniences and complications. But a day no less.

I'll tell you something, mate, it's one damn pain in the tummy, the neck, the feet and the ass, this thing they call Aids. And there are days when I wake up and wonder if I can stomach all this ghastly medication for the rest of my life. When I worry about what other innocuous-sounding, life-threatening, opportunistic discomforts lie in store. When I wonder if it's really worth all the drama. When I doubt, for a moment, whether or not I can possibly bear to go on *living with it*. And then I remember the other possibility: *Not* living with it. Not living at all.

HAVE I GOT MY SATISFACTION?
10 April 2005

YESTERDAY, I PICKED UP a dusty guitar and went out to buy a new D string to replace the one that had rusted, pling, as I lay dying. I have always sought solace in melody, and trusted it to bring out the lyrics from somewhere deep in my subconscious. Poems that write themselves. I know they're kinda corny, my songs. 'Oh, that dreadful folk music of yours!' Kate despairs. But who cares what Kate says? Different strokes, mate. And so, yesterday afternoon, I lit a reefer and plucked on a couple of strings, and this is what came out:

> *Two-year-olds might just provide*
> *Solutions to these existential*
> *Journeys of discovery*
> *Unsated curiosities*
> *And trying to find a melody*
> *That rings true for you*
>
> *So it's people that you bump into*
> *And folks who say that I would like to*
> *Meet you, understand you*
> *It's a random interaction*
> *A possible attraction*
> *With the huge risk of distraction*
> *Yes you know, guess you know it's true*

Can I relax? Will I relapse?
Are you quite sure that just perhaps
There's hope in all these remedies?
And a future in these memories?
I will risk a full recovery
But will you?

If I risk nothing, I risk everything
If I risk everything, I will have nothing

So it's one thing and another
All you sisters, brothers, mothers, lovers
And all the others that I never knew
And I'm checking my reactions
And deciphering these abstractions
Have I got my satisfaction?
And have you?

Come let's face up to statistics
And just try be realistic
I'm better off optimistic
And so are you
It's the only final reckoning
The truth forever beckoning
Did I get my satisfaction?
And did you?
And did you?

THE ART OF AFRICAN SHOPPING
22 April 2005

LAST NIGHT RAISED THE bar on beauty and happiness during my lifetime. We launched *The Art of African Shopping* in a clean, beautifully lit, contemporary gallery in Melrose Arch. The walls exploded with the potently hued Afro-futurist photographs I had created for the book with Alex's husband, Wendel. Colin, whom I hardly knew, had offered to do the flower arrangements. He asked for nothing in return: he was delighted just to be part of such an exciting project, he said. The results were an Afro-futurist's dream: forests of luminous red twigs, studded with the pinkest and yellowest Barberton daisies I've ever seen. How had he guessed that colours like that are my heroin?

The gallery's shelves were stacked with fifty framed illustrations I had drawn for the book. I remember crouching in pain, fiddling with tiny inky details and shadows; then digging deep into my memory for anecdotes of my life as a trader (another life – one of the many I have crammed into the past few decades); reading – when my arms were too weak and skinny to hold a heavy book; and writing, whenever I managed to sit upright. The fact that this rich rainbow of a book had been born during the darkest chapter of my life was indeed a miracle. And the fact that I had mounted the exhibition in a single day and had managed to remain on my feet to greet the 250 wonderful people who turned up that night was another. The fact that my father agreed to make a speech was the third.

Initially he had turned me down, assuring me that he would be too choked with tears to get through it, but eventually he came around. Little did I realise what forgotten evidence of my eclectic persona was lurking in the family archives. He produced my earliest piece of writing, a scrawl that had been discovered, pinned to the garden gate. 'If you look for me, you will not find me, because I am in disguise.' Hmmn. As I stood waiting in the wings, dressed up as the book's cover (a surreal, Afro-futurist figure in a screaming pink shirt, tie and white Baoule mask), I realised how little had changed.

Next up was a quite frightening photograph of a precocious, spectacled nine-year-old and some cringeworthy poems I had spewed up during my adolescence. There was an essay I had written at nineteen, titled 'Waddayagonnadowithyourlife?' which had fatefully proved rather accurate, and a note I had written Dad on his sixtieth birthday, which thanked him for the unlikely exposure my upbringing had afforded me to exotic images and ideas, and ended with the words 'Fuck soccer'. Dad spoke of my relentless ability to reinvent myself, and of the challenges we had all faced in the past two years, and he affirmed the miracle of our shared presence that evening. As promised, he brushed away the tears at moments and, as I looked up, I noticed that many members of the audience had joined him. When he introduced me, I pulled myself together and crept forward, holding the mask in front of my face, and began to speak.

There are times when the wearer becomes the mask, I said. *And there are times when the author becomes the book*. I removed the mask and continued. *But there is also a very remote risk that the reader becomes the book ... So don't say I didn't warn you. Don't blame me if you buy this book and you look in the mirror one morning and see that!* I pointed to the images on the walls ... *Or that! Stranger things have happened in Africa! So don't come grovelling with a lawsuit. Don't come crying for a refund.*

I have a story: Eighteen months ago, just before the launch of The Wonder Safaris *– at which many of you committed and supportive Afrophiles were present, my talented editor at Struik, Dominique le Roux, came to me with an idea for a new book: A guide to African art. Something the shopper could carry with them to a flea market to help them make sense of the overwhelming labyrinth of masks, cloths and traders' lies. It seemed a very good idea; there was just one tiny snag. I had full-blown Aids at the time. How was I to cover a continent when I couldn't leave my bed?*

Anyhow, as I lay dying, I gave it some thought. After some days, and with a little life in me from my mother's nourishing food and care, I felt strong enough to lift a hardcover tome, and began reading my way through my father's amazing collection of African art books. I read and read and read, and, in the process, I realised, in my morphined haze, that much of Dominique's good idea was already inside me! I had spent a decade travelling through twenty countries, writing stories, making sketches of objects I loved and working as a soul trader of African art and craft. I realised that I had already long begun to school myself in the Art of African Shopping, and I grasped quite magically, as one sometimes does in life, that what had seemed utterly impossible was indeed quite possible.

As I wrote, however, I realised that what I was holding in my hands was growing like an immense boil. What had started out as a few anecdotes and a little guide was swelling into a modest encyclopaedia of the continent's textiles, sculpture, jewellery, music, fashion, food and contemporary art. It was a rather ambitious task, considering my condition, which had by then come to various predicaments, including tuberculosis, cancer and bouts of debilitating chemotherapy. And yet somehow still possible.

What I didn't yet realise was just how healing the process of creating this book would prove. I'd crouch in pain, making more tiny sketches of the wonderful pieces in my own and my parents' home. The content of the book — the warm, organic of this continent's handmade objects and all the magical ingenuity involved in creating them — also proved a very good medicine. It was only much later that I realised, to my great surprise, that writing this book had saved my life.

I remember looking up at that point and seeing various grown men sobbing. I was astonished and deeply humbled, but I wasn't done yet.

There were a couple of doctors who played a part in this as well. I pointed to Dr D, who had turned up, and left out Dr S, who had not. *As did the unimaginable support of my parents, my sisters, and of course Alex, Katy, Roy, Bird, Ren, Teri, Zingi, Quen and many others. Ultimately, however, I cannot deny that, most of all, it was creating a book about these things I truly love that gave me a reason to stagger up in the morning.*

Although this book is not about mortality, you might encounter a shiver of it in the text. You might sense some urgency in the narrative. You might observe some detail and fragility in the sketches you see around you. The photographs Wendel and I created possess the dramatic colour of optimism I required to get me through those dark days. These wondrous African things made me want to live. And we are blessed to live on a continent where these wondrous things are all around us.

And so, as I have written on the book's back cover: Come let us decipher the enigmatic geometry of raffia velvets. Let us peer behind the strange, abstract features of Basonge masks. Let us sway to the captivating rhythms of ancient Berber chants and drown ourselves in the rapturous aromas of ylang-ylang flowers and steaming plates of yassa. Come, let our rich and sensual pilgrimage through the world's most mysterious continent begin.

I have tried to sum up my feelings in a little song, I proceeded. *You may recognise the tune or the sentiment.*

Raindrops in Togo and sandstorms in Mali
Plates of aloco and bowls of ugali
Djembes, mirimbas and koras with strings
These are a few of my favourite things

Kubas and kentes and mudcloths and kangas
Dancing and drumming beneath a full nyanga
Boubous and fezzes and fine Tuareg rings
These are a few of my favourite things

So I shop more
I should stop more
Am I going mad?
And then I remember they're African things
And then I don't feel so bad

Zulu and Ewe, Baoule and Basonge
Berber and Tuareg, Maasai and Makonde
Mint tea and reefer and Zanzibar flings
These are a few of my favourite things

On my journey, I get weary
I start feeling sad
And then I remember these African things
And then I don't feel so ... so bad

I worried that a few notes might have been out of key, but I didn't care. I had sung from the gut and it appeared that everyone had heard and felt where it was coming from, but still, I wasn't quite done.

This book is about some very ancient heritage — about the tremendous creative accomplishments of this continent. And if there's anyone here who thinks that tribal art is somehow passé or not contemporary enough for your tastes, well, you could leave now, 'cos baby, if it was good enough for Picasso, then it's good enough for you.

That said, you know that writing a book is a journey. And the thing with a journey is that you end somewhere different from where you started. As I reached the end of this written journey I had come to think very deeply about the notion of Afro-futurism — about imagining the arts of this continent in the year 2050. I realised that the possibilities of this continent's creativity are as endless and beautiful as the dawning of an African sky. And that Björk might just turn out not to be an Icelandic geisha but a young Xhosa man called Zingi, who happens to be my housemate, and I will leave you with some evidence. As they might say in the year 2050 ... Björk, woza!

At which point, Zingi made his way through the audience, dressed in an antique oriental kimono, with a Basonge mask strapped to his belly and traditional medicinal paste smeared on his face, wailing plaintively in Xhosa: the perfectly appropriate muddle of race, gender, genre and ethnicity for such an event. As his soothing African lullaby morphed into a haunting Björk aria he had chosen for me, the audience was mesmerised.

We'd pulled it off. Mom, Alli, Dad, Wendel, Michael, the gallery owner, Zing, me and these two feet. We had done it, and whoever wanted one, sure deserved a puff or two of the dangerous, home-grown weed my sister had brought along. I still shiver in horror at what I might have inscribed in the books that were subsequently presented to me, but I can tell you, these were far from innocuous inscriptions. I seem to remember writing, 'Get real!' in one copy, but hey, he'd brought me a pen, the uptight clown, what did he expect?

Still, I made sure, despite all the ensuing administrative drama, to savour every precious moment of this magical night that will undoubtedly prove far more memorable than my bar mitzvah. I glanced at the gallery as I exited, freezing that hopeful, perfect vision of colour, Africa and tomorrow in my memory. And in my ecstasy, I paused to acknowledge what I might have missed out on, had I let go in those rare moments when the proximity of death and its promise of release from pain had almost seemed appealing.

JESUS DRAG II
24 April 2005

YES, IT'S TRUE: DURING the time I thought death was near, it seemed funny, with my ribcage poking skeletal through my pale skin and my sparrow-leg arms, to entertain and horrify my friends with the now notorious incident of Jesus Drag. Little did I realise how eerily this impersonation would return to haunt me as I began to feel better.

This is a difficult one to write – messy and complicated, but true nevertheless. And there is no point in me writing a memoir that is not the truth, the whole truth and nothing but a bunch of reconsidered lies.

The thing is this: lately, as I step out into the world, I do so carefully, but I also take care not to forget that the universe is still a big, ripe yellow peach, bursting with the sweet juice of possibility. That I might yet encounter wondrous people in unlikely places and circumstances. That I might even meet someone I'd want to love, or someone who just might be insane, brave and special enough to risk some real, enduring intimacy with such a complicated lad as meself.

I'm a package. I know I am – what with these plastic teeth and sore feet and sixty pills a day. But hey, I was a package before I got Aids. Before I was gay. Before I started going to ridiculous places and writing about them. Before I developed such obscure tastes. I was a freak the day I was born. (Given that I didn't exit her womb with fifteen toes, Mom prefers the term 'free spirit', but we've settled on 'individual'.) And the past thirty-six years would have probably been far less interesting had it been otherwise. So, what are the odds? You don't try, you'll never know.

I do my best to remember what good, simple things are also in that package, and not to allow fear to form a hard crust around my heart. *I'm better off optimistic / And so are you.* There are astonishing beings in this universe and I want to meet them. I will engage rather than retreat. I'm alive, dammit!

So it's people that you bump into / And folks who say that I would like to / Meet you, understand you / It's a random interaction / A possible attraction / With the huge risk of distraction / Guess you know / Yes you know it's true …

And so I have ventured *out*. After so many months inside, I am enjoying the thrill of outside, even in the cool, grey, wet, Highveld autumn. And I am happening on wonderfull surprises. In the process, however, I have observed a strange resonance in many of my encounters. I meet all sorts of people. The arthritic old woman sitting next to me in the blood-test queue. People who tell me they have passed on my books to family members in prison or in rural areas, where they have been passed from hut to hut. Wow! Black economic empowerment kids, speeding past me on too much cocaine. Wise women. Men. *Men* again.

It is in the spirit of full disclosure that I find myself divulging this whole ghastly story to them, like a bucket of confessional vomit – just in case they don't realise who or what they're dealing with, and, most often, the universe rewards me generously for my openness. Although some people are initially repulsed or frightened by the Aids in me, they generally come around. There are some who tell me how deeply my courage has affected them. They tell me I'm a teacher. A survivor. That meeting me has somehow changed their lives. Is it my story of near death and near resurrection that has them confusing me with some kind of saviour? Or is it just my hair – which has grown out rather nicely since chemo? I don't know. But every now and then, it seems, people seem to confuse me with someone that I'm not. They tell me that we were meant to meet for a reason. And sometimes that's the last I hear from them. (What was the reason?)

I am always flattered, honoured even, by such impromptu declarations, but lately I have also grown a little wary of them. I see no great heroism in this tale. Looking back, the progression of events is quite clear to me. I cowered in denial until finally, standing at the door of death, the people who love me persuaded me to face my greatest fears. It is thanks to them that I scraped up the courage to do so, far too late, far too long after my flesh had begun wasting away at the mercy of a virus I had made no effort to educate myself about. As the seas became stormier, I clung with frail fingers to a rapidly sinking raft, and when I finally realised I was drowning, I gasped and spluttered for my breath for no other reason than that I realised how very much I adored being alive. At that moment, would you have done anything differently?

And so I have come to wonder if by placing me on such an inappropriate pedestal folks are not saving themselves the horror of actually investing in some closeness with me. 'You are a shining example,' people tell me. Who wants to be a fucking example? I'm the real thing. But perhaps it is easier to revere than to love. It requires far less personal involvement. Less tedious baggage checking. Less mess. It is safer. We step forward tentatively, constantly balancing the scales of danger and safety. *If I risk nothing, I risk everything / If I risk everything, I will have nothing.*

I don't want to be revered. Often, like many of us, I have thought of this as something appealing, but, sitting now, alone, and writing this passage, I know that such adulation is a cold and lonely place to be. In truth I would prefer something much less glorious, but far more challenging. I want to retain my faith in love, and like all of us, I want to be loved. I want good things in my life, for I know that, in the end, it is the good things that last, and the lasting things that matter most.

I don't want to be anyone's Jesus. But it would be good to be someone's Adam again sometime. When I performed for Alex that dark night, I was only joking: a moment of irreverent burlesque to distract me from the bleak, paralysing terror of dying. I should have known better. I should have known that such profane dalliance would ultimately come back to mess with me. I should have known that impersonating Christ might one day result in some unintended vocation, and that it might land up being much more of a drag than I'd ever imagined.

I met someone a few nights ago. Within five minutes I had uttered the words Aids, cancer and tuberculosis. Within the following five, he had told me this: If I fell in love with someone who was HIV-positive, I would want to contract the virus from them and *share* it – but only if I knew we'd be together forever.

Are you insane? I shivered. Firstly, *nothing* is forever. Secondly, do you have any idea what you'd be letting yourself in for?

'Yes, of course I do,' he replied. 'I'm an HIV counsellor.'

Thirdly, I was horrified.

I'd been warned about such people. *Bug-chasers* they call them. Folks who get tangled up in some misguided empathy or shady masochistic desire. People who think HIV is the name of some swanky, risqué club, reserved for the select few with miserable cell counts. People who feel excluded from the attention that people with Aids might receive. Sick, dark people who think opportunistic infections are a birthday party.

They scare me – them bug-chasers. Perhaps they remind me of myself. Perhaps, subconsciously, I was some kind of twisted bug-chaser a few years ago. I hope not. But I know that I will not be chased. I live with the horror that I might have unwittingly transmitted this virus to someone else, just as someone must have passed it on to me, and I have made a conscious choice not to expose anyone to that risk again – no matter how desperately they might want me to. I will live the rest of my life within a condom of consequence. Never again will I truly feel the erotic intimacy of skin inside skin. But I will feel skin against skin. I will allow myself to touch and to be touched. For as long as a heart still thumps in this chest.

Recently, a close friend of mine was utterly horrified that I would even consider dating someone again. 'In your condition!' he raged. 'Don't you realise? No sex is safe! I was so horrified by what happened to you that *I* have taken a vow of celibacy, and *you* are out there, carrying on, up to your old ways.'

No, I protested. I am up to new ways. You may choose complete abstinence, but I don't. I am very, very careful. I declare my status to the world. I do not give people the opportunity to worry about the strange way I walk or my patchy skin. I intercept their uncertainty with my scary truth. And I do more than that: I make it *my* responsibility to protect them, with the knowledge that they might be as lost and frightened as I once was.

Over the past decade, medical science has changed Aids from a death sentence to a life sentence of coloured tablets, blood-tests and uncertainty. A most merciful probation? Indeed. But, I take the time to remember that this sentence is only a consequence, and not a punishment, and that it has not been passed with any condition of solitary confinement – for a life sentence of loneliness is no better than a death sentence. If we do not have one another, we have nothing. It is an honour to make a difference in anyone's life, but it is also a great pleasure to allow anyone to make a difference in mine.

I will still hold and I will still be held. But I will not be anyone's Jesus: I will be flawed and fragile and human – whenever and wherever I find the opportunity. It is the very least and the very most I could ever hope for – for me and for anyone else whose path might happen to meander across mine.

TRANNIE PUNKS WILL RULE THE WORLD
29 May 2005

During the past month, my life has been haunted with recurrent but reassuring flashes of familiarity. I have been spending much more time at my house, away from the safety zone of Mom and Dad's intensive care, and forging on with the mundane obligations of making a living and having some kind of life. I have experienced moments of deep relief during this time, going to exhibition openings, movies and events again – sweet, small pleasures that I always took for granted, but there have been other moments, lying in my own bed, in my own home, in dark, eerie solitude, when the reality of living with Aids has felt more terrifying than ever. Is this really your life? I ask. Are you still absolutely certain this hasn't all been a horrible dream? I listen for voices, but hear none, until finally the pain and silence provide me with cold, incontestable certainty.

For the past two years, my life has been governed by crisis. Every waking moment has been consumed with fighting this disease, and in a strange way, that fight has sheltered and distracted me from the real issues that face me. As I battled for my survival, I put my dreams on hold. The banal challenges of existence dimmed into insignificance, shadowed by the overwhelming challenge of waging a war for survival inside my body. Now, as my life hobbles its way into some semblance of what it once was, I see everything with spooky clarity again, and I grasp that those same challenges remain. While this experience may have left me a little wiser, it hasn't solved anything. Essentially, I am the same person, with the same bundle of hopes and joys and fears as I was before this nightmarish journey inside me began.

At moments I catch myself off guard – sobbing rivers in the midst of some truly corny TV movie or *Oprah*. I know it's not the television: I know there's some deep sadness inside me, and that, in the past, that feeling always sent me running scared into all the wrong places, but I've got better at it. I allow myself the occasional blue day when I need it, for I know that its only solutions are patience and stamina – getting through the sadness and trusting that there will always be more joy and excitement beyond it. Life has many colours, and without the blue, how would I recognise the pink or the orange?

I do my best to be tolerant, but my mates tell me I'm not very good at it. Try as I might, I don't tolerate *intolerance* very well. So, what does that make me? Aren't I supposed to accommodate people who might be racist, sexist, homophobic or even virophobic? To make space for them in the world and allow them their prejudices no matter how much they rile me? Well, I can't – not without reading them their rights.

I can't say I have much time for mediocrity either. There's just too much spontaneity and originality on the prowl to bother. Deep down, each of us has the potential to rise above bland ordinariness and exude a vibrant individuality, I figure. Some rise and some don't. So, hey, maybe I'm not so tolerant. So shoot me. I'm sure some people aren't crazy about me either. So what you gonna do? At the risk of sounding a little preachy: Not everyone's gonna love ya.

I wrote to Marcos recently, expressing the difficulties I'd been encountering lately, convincing people that I am really quite simple and easy-going – only I knew that just when they thought they'd found a pleasant chap to watch videos with, I'd come strolling in casually, painted green. He called me from Brazil and we chuckled at the hopelessness of attempting anything so ludicrous. He'd seen me painted both blue and white, but the thought of green had him laughing hysterically all the way from São Paulo. So I was still a Martian. What else was new?

* * *

A couple of weeks ago, while sifting through the chaotic Lost and Found columns of my cupboards and drawers, I happened on an unfamiliar object some anonymous squatter had serendipitously left behind at some point: a microphone. Shriek! A miracle. It wasn't five minutes before Zingi and I had plugged our new toy into the stereo and were belting out shameless duets with all our favourite divas. It was karaoke, only better. Now Zingi could croon away with Bette Midler, and I could rasp along with Tom Waits, in full stereophonic glory.

Somehow, despite the mysterious disappearance of much of the old drag trunk, one rather tatty beige wig had survived, and there were still plenty defenceless garments, lying about, susceptible to spectacular reinvention. So, if it wasn't a skirt on the shoulders or a blazer turned inside out, it was a sari going as a turban or a rogue stiletto placed precariously on the head and a gala performance in the living room, mike in hand. You know? Like ya do.

Consequently, any unsuspecting callers, hoping for a quiet, relaxed visit, would now be subjected to a smorgasbord of brazen, full-blast exhibitionism. As it's turned out, however, the regular Duets sessions have proved rather popular. Generally, it's no longer than half an hour before a couple of guests sneak off to their cars to retrieve their favourite CDs and proceed to plunge into their own stellar, impromptu recitals. The variety of guests has revealed a universe of eclectic musical tastes, ranging from old French bistro tunes to Brazilian rock to cheesy, mascara-dripping R&B. Who'd have thought such closet megastars were twinkling among us?

The return of such silliness to my life has been deeply comforting for me. The fact that, for all its seriousness, life can still make me laugh so hard that my dentures hurt, and that anyone with a voice, no matter how dismally out of tune, can still sprinkle a little glitter about and transform him- or herself into a global celebrity on an ordinary Tuesday evening, has left me feeling profoundly reassured about the universe.

I have lost many things over the past couple of years, but I am delighted to report that, while this virus may have invaded almost every cell in my body, my sense of humour, mischief and spontaneity has remained miraculously intact. How cheering it has been to grasp that you can have Aids and still position a plastic flower arrangement on your head, should the spirit move you. That you can have an incurable disease and still be a transvestite or a punk, should you feel so inclined. A Trannie Punk, if you like.

Last night, I set myself the ambitious task of preparing a dinner party, for Alex, Wendel, Zingi and some new friends. We washed down bowls of spicy tom yam soup with shrimp and retired to the fireside for glasses of Zingi's glühwein. It seemed a good moment to introduce a relatively unexplored musical genre I had been toying with. 'Drag Folk,' I announced. (Yes, Kate, that dreadful folk music again, but tinged with a little glam tack this time round.) Think Bob Dylan in pearls. A niche market to be sure, but certainly not yet saturated.

My guests were persuaded – as if they'd had much choice – and so I combed out the nasty beige wig, scrounged for a smear of cheap lipstick, and sat myself down, guitar resting precariously on a ruffled, chiffon knee, and proceeded to deliver my Drag Folk debut: a drunken, throaty ditty, modestly entitled, *Trannie Punks Will Rule the World*.

> *I've got a shirtwaister dress that once was new*
> *I've got a single, silver, strapped, stiletto Jimmy Choo*
> *I've got a diamanté brooch that I stole from you*
> *'Cos being a boy's a tricky thing to do*
> *It's true*
> *Being a boy's a tricky thing to do*
>
> *I've got a pile of someone else's hair on top of my head*
> *I've got my lips painted silver and my eyes blood red*
> *I've got a black lace skirt going as a sleeve instead*
> *'Cos being a boy's a tricky thing to do*

Don't you ...
Secretly like tricky things too?

I know that some people think it's a drag
And that my friends all swear that I will never get a shag
But I got my Nokia, my frock here, and my favourite bag
So what the hell am I supposed to do?
It's just that being a girl's a silly thing to do
Don't you ...
Secretly like silly things too?

Fat rich accountants will swallow the world
So get your eyelashes and body paint and Josephine's curls
And then you runway, that and this way
And you make 'em listen, Girl
You tell them ... Trannie Punks will rule the world
You go Girl!
One day Trannie Punks will rule ... the world.

IF I HAD KNOWN, WOULD I HAVE ...?

5 June 2005

AIDS IS A RIDDLE. It is invisible and yet it is everywhere, all around us, in people we love, in me. It doesn't matter if you are HIV-positive or negative. The world has Aids. And if you give a shit about the world, you have it too.

As the statistics attest, South Africa, with its legacy of apartheid and long-engrained culture of secrets and lies, was all the more vulnerable when the pandemic struck, and thousands of lives have been lost to shame and ignorance. And if *this* disease cannot teach us something very deep ... about compassion, I doubt there is anything on this planet that will.

It is true. In theory, the rules of prevention are fairly clear. Practise safer sex. Use a condom. Don't kiss anyone with open sores in their mouths. But the realities are far more complex. Everyone hates condoms. They stick. They break. They don't always roll out smoothly like a banana peel. And they rarely fail to interrupt the intoxicating, erotic ecstasy of the moment.

In theory, the rules of courtship are equally simple. Abstain from indiscriminate sex. Stay faithful to a nurturing, monogamous relationship. But what if you don't happen to be in some fucking nurturing, monogamous relationship? What then? Then, of course, it's all much trickier. Being young, alive, and charged at times with some angry foolish bravado, it's easy enough to get lost, as you clamber through the thrilling labyrinth of life. Lost in drugs, alcohol or the comfort of strangers. And sometimes, in that lostness, it's easy enough to forget that this invisible thing called Aids is real and that it can really gobble up your immune system, your body, your freedom, your independence and sometimes your life. But Aids is real. And it's also real, real scary.

As far as the local prevention campaigns are concerned, those already infected with the virus are a generation lost. By necessity, they have written us off for dead and focus only on the young people of this country who have miraculously managed to remain negative. '2010. I want to be there,' the campaign runs – regardless of anyone who might not be there, or who might need a whole lot of help in getting there. It seems a cruel but perfectly understandable stance for that particular sector of this country's hugely flawed crusade.

From the very beginning of my tormented relationship with Aids, I made peace with all the choices I had made. Like most of the people close to me, I was fiercely resolute not to wrestle with the demons of regret. The past is past and all that matters is the present and the future. But now, given the unimaginably grave consequences I have suffered over the past two years, there is a voice inside me that nags for re-evaluation. 'If I had known?' it cries. 'Would I have …?'

… And so, I must journey all the way back to a very dark place in my memory. To some nowhere, running into the arms of someone – anyone who might save me from the momentary horrors of loneliness. I must place myself in the throes of desire, to that critical instant, when my dick was throbbing so insanely with ecstasy it was ready to burst. I must place myself at the boundaries of safety, ready to trespass into the thrilling territory of dangerous abandon that lay just beyond them. Now, years later, I stand at that border post and I wonder. If I had known, would I have …?

If I'd had the slightest inkling of the sheer, interminable agony that I was to endure – the helplessness, the humiliating dependency, the frightening uncertainties, the fierce battles with cancer and tuberculosis, the loss of my body weight, my hair, the very teeth in my mouth – would I have crossed that line?

I cannot answer that question. If the choice had been that clear or simple, I am sure I would have found the strength within me to restrain myself. But it wasn't. If the world had been less secretive about the horrifying realities of this disease, perhaps I would have been wiser as to the gravity of that crossing. But it wasn't. That was another time, and another me, with another idea of what really mattered in a crazy, bewildering, grown-up world. And regardless of the drastic, unexpected and all-encompassing turn my life would take after a sunny winter's day in August 2003, I must still take full responsibility for who I was and the choices I made at that time of my life.

I do not know how to end this memoir, but the end does not matter. Maybe there's another book about Aids in me. Maybe there's a tombstone waiting. But that doesn't matter either. What matters is a subtle but fundamental shift inside me – for, in making this decision, I absolve myself of any trace of guilt or regret. And yet, this absolution does not come without its own incontestable condition of accountability. For if I am to own my past, I must take full ownership and responsibility for my present. I must accept everything that has happened and everything that is still to come, regardless of any sadness, tragedy or pain. I must find the courage to keep fighting – to keep my body alive and my spirit on fire, without risking an instant of self-pity. I must welcome the extraordinary growth and the profound, eternal lessons of existence that this journey has offered me, and continue to treasure each single, blessed thing the weather happens to blow into my life.

It is my great wish to make more wondrous safaris in

the course of my life. Journeys create journeys, and I hope to make many more of them, both inside and out. This virus hasn't wacked me yet, but if I'm not very careful, boredom or apathy might. I'm doing okay at the moment. I'm not fine, but I'm okay. Some folks who meet me don't have a clue what I've been through, and I'm happy to fill them in if it's relevant, but it's not *all* about Aids. I'm just as happy yakking on about fashion or Africa or plotting a cultural revolution as I am busting the viral silence.

Life is still a great voyage for me, rich with miracles and surprises. I'm walking better now, but I know I can traverse the universe without taking a single step. There are 747s in my mind, just waiting to take flight. I have my suitcase ready, packed with precious memories and a few slivers of wisdom and experience, and I'm still pretty much always up for an adventure.

So c'mon, let's go …

Do you have any comments, suggestions or feedback
about this book or any other Zebra Press titles?
Contact us at **talkback@zebrapress.co.za**